FLOWER READINGS

FLOWER READINGS

Discover your true self through the
ancient art of Flower Psychometry

SUZY CHIAZZARI

INDEX COMPILED BY ANN GRIFFITHS

FLOWER ILLUSTRATIONS BY JANE NORMAN

SAFFRON WALDEN
THE C.W. DANIEL COMPANY LIMITED

First published in Great Britain in 2000
by The C.W. Daniel Company Limited,
1 Church Path, Saffron Walden,
Essex CB10 1JP, United Kingdom

ISBN 0 85207 338 0

We wish to thank *The British Homoeopathic Journal* for permission
to use The rhythm of Venus illustration on page 55.

Designed & illustrated by Jane Norman
Produced in association with Book Production Consultants plc,
25–27 High Street, Chesterton, Cambridge CB4 1ND
Typeset by Cambridge Photosetting Services
Printed by Hillman Printers (Frome) Ltd, England

CONTENTS

Introduction vii

PART 1 1

The language of flowers, Past wisdom – future health, Flowermancy,
Evolving towards simplicity, Spiritual evolution, Flower emblems of the world,
Inter-species communication, Flowers for self-reflection,
How your flower reflection can heal your life, Energy medicine,
The energy centres of the body, Flower essence therapy, Healing with flowers

PART 2 19

Finding your flower, Tuning in to the natural world,
Contacting the Deva of the flower, Finding your flower using colour photographs
and drawings, Decoding the energy patterns, Giving a flower reading,
Understanding energy patterns in relation to your inner state,
Flower families and their central themes, Habitat – a key to your
present circumstances, How your flower mimics your body language,
Shape – the key to your state of mind, The energy of number, Insect energy

PART 3 63

The healing power of your flower, Transformative energy, Spirals, Flowers as
mandalas, Colour, Texture – the key to the way healing takes place, Aroma,
Preserving flower energy, Flower ceremonies, Flowers as meditation aids,
Creating a healing essence from your flower, Taking flower essences,
Healing themes of different flower essences of the world, Flowers linked to the
five natural elements, Four case studies of flower readings

PART 4 103

Healing the planet, Network of light energy, The ladder of ascent,
Flower colours in relation to your life's work, Flowers as an aid to evolution,
Our crystalline planet, Healing for the new era, The spiritual renaissance,
Flower reading chart

Further reading & useful addresses 117

Index 120

Introduction

There is no such thing as an ordinary flower. Each flower is a masterpiece of subtle beauty, form and scent. All flowers hold a mystery which unfolds as it develops into new forms and reveals new features of interest and beauty to those who love them. By loving flowers you are naturally linked with the divine because you are not bound by time and place. Your sensitivity connects you to other lovers, past and present, and to millions of other people around the world. Flowers unify through love.

In the words of fellow flower-lover John Ruskin (1819–1900): '*We cannot fathom the mystery of a single flower, nor is it intended that we should; but that the pursuit of science should constantly be betrayed by the love of beauty, and accuracy of knowledge by tenderness of emotion.*'

Looking at a flower is like holding up a mirror to your soul in which you can see your life more clearly; for in its shape, aroma and colour we can find parallels to our lives. Your favourite flower can reveal a great deal about you. In this book of Flower Readings you will discover how they can be used to bring about wonderful healing on all levels.

Flowers are not only beautiful, they have always been used for medicinal purposes. Their powers have been reputed not only for ailments of the body, but also of the mind and spirit. This knowledge has developed into many systems of healing as varied as homoeopathy, aromatherapy, herbalism and meditation. While we can obtain flower medicines from many different practitioners, it is also possible to experience direct healing from the flower itself.

Around the world, flowers have always been revered as magical, and people over the centuries have practised mystical rituals using their power. One such ancient system is known as 'flower psychometry'.

In the past, the knowledge and ability to interpret the messages held in flowers were exclusively held by priests and healers, but anyone can learn to use this knowledge. In order to discover this healing magic for yourself, you first have to locate the right flower and then discover what healing power it has for you.

All you have to do is to take time intuitively to find a flower in a garden or, if this is not possible, to select a flower from a good selection of drawings or photographs. This flower will contain personal information about you and hold the exact pattern of healing energy you need.

In this book I will show you how flowers can be used in an intimate way to help bring out the best in you and guide you towards a happier and healthier life. The flower will reflect both your inner state of health whilst allowing you to see the bigger picture – your life in relation to your place in the world. Rather than telling you your fate, it will help you see potential so that you are empowered to create your own future.

Flower Readings will take you through the enjoyable process of 'reading' your flower, using a simple set of tools that interprets the energy patterns reflected in its form, colour and scent. A flower reading can be beneficial to anyone, of any age, at any time. You do not have to be ill or depressed in order to benefit as a flower reading can be equally helpful during times of change or when an important decision has to be made.

Giving a flower reading is not only fun, it is also profound. As the name suggests, flower psychometry links flowers to our psyche and we can use this art in a very positive way. By seeing your life more clearly, the flower can reveal inner strengths and talents that you may not be using. The colours, shapes and patterns in your flower will also point to the path you should be following in order to reach your full potential. By following your true life's work you can improve your quality of life and enjoy a feeling of fulfilment.

Your chosen flower will reflect both your strengths and your weaknesses and help you identify negative mental and emotional patterns that may be holding you back. Once the area of disharmony is revealed, you can then use the healing vibrations held in the flower to bring your life into balance.

Flowers contain healing energy. I like to think of them as guardian angels who care and guide us. Every person has a flower guardian which is perfect in itself and can support and help us at any time. These spirits also maintain the connection and balance between the different kingdoms on earth.

The changes a flower brings is different from other forms of medicine in that it is able to bring about deep healing at soul level. The spirit of a flower helps us to feel whole and connected so that we become at peace with ourselves and the world. When this happens, different areas of our psyche come into balance and this harmony is also reflected in our life.

I believe that if we returned to this much more direct and simple form of healing many of our ailments and troubles would disappear. In *Flower*

Readings I hope to demonstrate how such a simple thing as a single flower can provide both a personal diagnosis and the exact prescription for restoring both internal and external harmony.

Most of all I hope that by reading and following the steps described in this book it helps develop your personal connection with the natural world and enables you to see flowers in a new and wonderful way. A flower is not only beautiful on the outside but has a radiant inner beauty – let it reflect yours too.

PART 1

The language of flowers

Past wisdom – future health

Flowermancy

Evolving towards simplicity

Spiritual evolution

Flower emblems of the world

Inter-species communication

Flowers for self-reflection

How your flower reflection can heal your life

Energy medicine

The energy centres of the body

Flower essence therapy

Healing with flowers

The language of flowers

Flowers have always been the most important gift of beauty in our perilous and often drab world. From the earliest ages, plants have been endowed with meanings and mystic powers until they have become inextricably woven into the folklore of all countries. The pagan priests set flowers apart for their gods just as the early Christian monks dedicated them to their saints. Together with their spiritual reputations, plants were also esteemed to be the only effective cures for many of our physical ailments. So, it is not surprising that we still have a deep feeling for these wonders of nature. Flowers represent a gift from the heart. Most people would say they would find a gift of flowers or even a single bloom more touching than a more expensive gift.

Long before the written word, flowers were used as a form of symbolic communication. The bouquets and posies of our ancestors were chosen not so much for their beauty as for the messages they could convey. Oriental traditions and many other ancient cultures are rich in flower imagery, while the language of flowers in the British Isles goes back to pre-Christian times. The interest in the messages of flowers continued into the Middle Ages and later was adopted and modified by the Victorians. During the 19th century, many books were published explaining the language of flowers and these were studied and used when making floral gifts.

Not only have we used flowers to communicate with one another, there is also a history of folklore using flowers for inner communication in the form of 'flowermancy' and flower psychometry. Today flower readings can be used for self-development and a greater understanding of our deep inner feelings and desires of which we may be unaware.

Past wisdom – future health

With each new year we are reminded of the importance of natural rhythms, for each day and each season follows the next in a continuous cycle. We live in a world of limits, and we need these constraints, just as a river needs its banks in order to flow towards the sea. Going with the flow of nature, cherishing the best of what we have and what we have inherited from the past can help our lives flow purposefully and smoothly. Rather than making a bonfire of everything which has gone before, we need to look to the profound wisdom of others who have made the difficult journey before us. Winston Churchill said that the further we look into the past, the further we can see into the future so by understanding the age old symbolism of flowers we can rediscover the clarity and simplicity of this natural healing tool and adapt it to our modern needs.

Flowermancy

Not only do flowers hold healing magic, they can also help us spiritually. This more esoteric use of flowers is known as flower psychometry.

Flower psychometry is a form of earth magic. In its most ancient form it uses all sorts of flowers and plants in prediction rituals and customs such as foreseeing your fortune in love, health or wealth. Most of this knowledge has been lost, but remnants survive. Children still pick dandelions and blow off the fluff, saying, 'he loves me, he loves me not, he loves me'. It is thought that if you count the number of puffs it takes to blow off all the seeds, this will tell you the number of years it will take for you to marry.

In one form of flower psychometry, once you have found the right flower, you allow it to go to seed. You then harvest the seed and speak to it about your problem before planting it. As the plant grows and changes, your problem will become transformed into something new and positive. The way I use flowermancy, however, is not concerned with using flowers as portents – We can use certain flowers in a much more intimate way to help us identify problem areas in our life.

To me, flower psychometry (as the name suggests), links flowers to our psyche and we can use it to mirror our state of health and identify aspects within our being that are out of balance. So, the flower you choose will give you an over-view of your life so you can see your situation in context. I call the process of discovering the message a flower has for you as a 'flower reflection reading'. Not only can a flower help us build up a picture of who we really are, it can also help us find areas of our life that we can change, while at the same time identifying circumstances that are beyond our control.

Evolving towards simplicity

Plants made their appearance on earth millions of years ago. Although animal life in a very basic form existed before plants made their appearance, these organisms remained dormant while the plants developed and evolved. We can therefore look upon plants as the wise sages of the earth from whom we can learn a great deal.

All life on earth is in continual motion, with a universal quest towards perfection. On a physical level this applies to the simplest rock formation as well as to the bodies of the higher mammals. Every kingdom is part of the cosmos and its natural movement is back towards unity with the divine. Leonardo da Vinci (*The Notebooks 1508–1518*) has this to say about nature: '*Human subtlety will never devise an invention more beautiful, more simple, or more direct than does nature, because in her inventions nothing is lacking, and nothing is superfluous.*'

In the plant kingdom, the flowering plant is the most highly evolved. Today we are fortunate enough to enjoy flowers representing many different stages of evolution. Some plants – for example, ferns – remain in their prehistoric state, while others have changed and modified over the millennia. As the growth and development of flowers follow universal laws we can conclude that all living things are evolving towards a similar state of purity and simplicity. When we look at the colour, shape and perfume of flowers through millions of years, we find that the continual changes all involve refinement and simplification. Many petals unite to form simple star shapes, while the colours become more iridescent and the perfume more ethereal. In flowers we find the simple message of unification of purpose towards perfection.

In the sea we have another excellent example of evolution towards simplicity. Dolphins and whales have evolved and adapted perfectly to their watery environment. These highly intelligent and adaptable mammals have a sleek and simple shape, perfectly suited to manoeuvring through water. Their senses, too, have become refined, so that they have developed sensory capabilities perfectly suited to the skills they require. In fact, the dolphin has been in existence far longer than we have and it can be argued that they are therefore as evolved – if not more so – than ourselves.

On land, human beings consider themselves the most highly evolved creatures in the animal kingdom but our physiological evolutionary changes have been slow. In fact, our bodies have changed little over thousands of years. Although our brains have increased in size, our development has been almost exclusively external through our ability to create more and more complex tools. If we were to meet one of our human ancestors, we would find that, except for the language and cultural differences, we have a great deal in common. There would not be many things we could do better than our ancient relatives.

Although the evolutionary process takes place over thousands of years, each one of us experiences a speeded-up version of this fantastic transformation. It is remarkable that the modern human embryo still traces the whole of our evolution from our watery beginnings through various stages of animal forms until finally our human body emerges.

Many people believe that, rather than evolving, we have lost many of our innate abilities – such as telepathy and sensitivity to electrical and magnetic vibrations. There are a few people left who still remain sensitive to electromagnetic energy and can sense the energy created by thunderstorms and earthquakes before they happen. It seems that the more we distance ourselves from the natural world the less sensitive we become.

One of the talents of people who live close to nature is their ability to read natural signs. In many places today, folklore still exists that helps farmers and country people to predict the weather and other natural phenomena by the colours in the sky, and the movements of animals and birds. This knowledge has been passed down in stories, celebrations and rituals.

Unfortunately, as we spend more than eighty per cent of our lives indoors, we are rapidly losing our connection with nature. Science and technology are proving not to have the answers that will reduce stress and provide a better quality of life. Technology is, instead, hastening our distance from our spirit and the part of us that connects to the cosmic forces. We are, indeed, working against nature and are making our lives more complicated rather than working towards singularity of purpose and togetherness. In our highly complex world, we once again need to find the simplicity of living and, by doing so, we will find the peace and contentment that is eluding us.

Flowers reflect the human search for meaning, for no matter how our life unfolds, do we not long to have a life as beautiful and true to itself as a flower?

Flowers are the gift nature has provided to help us regain connection with our true selves, for in flowers we can see our soul's reflection. Flower psychometry can help us to see our state of being at any time and to appreciate our individual beauty and potential. Flowers reflect our human search for meaning in our lives: they can help us to see again when we have lost our way. Through their subtle vibrations they waken our hearts and nourish our spirit so we can become whole.

Pam Brown in her writings of 1928 sums up the gifts of flowers like this: 'They grow among desolation. They shroud the scars of war. They grant a haven to the desolate. They bring hope to those who are injured or ill. They comfort the bereaved. They mark remembrance. They cheer a city yard and suburban garden. They defy the machine. They are lights in the darkness. They are the promise of renewal. They are life.'

Spiritual evolution

In the garden we can create a sanctuary where we can contact our soul's impulses and learn the secret of life itself. Gardens are symbolic of our consciousness as they are planned and controlled in contrast to the natural untamed countryside. We fill our consciousness with our own thoughts and feelings just as we fill our gardens with flowers which represent our hopes and dreams.

Evolution is not only about physical survival, it also embraces the spirit of the universe. At a spiritual level we need to evolve and grow, purifying our body, mind and spirit so we can connect with the divine.

This is not a new idea for as the Italian poet and philosopher Dante (1265-1321) wrote in his work, *The Divine Comedy*, the strongest desire of everything, and the first thing implanted by nature, is to return to its source.

The energy flowing through a plant moves upwards and condenses as the flower develops so that it becomes a spiritual force which can uplift the spirit. The flower holds the potential to achieve perfection and we can enter the embrace of its mystical power by our ability to appreciate such beauty. When going into a garden of flowers on a fresh morning you can experience for a time a feeling of perfect peace and contentment. Each flower gives its colour, grace and perfume which enriches us with the consummation of its beauty.

We have such a close intuitive relationship with flowers that we often instinctively identify with certain flowers. Most people have favourite flowers which reflect their own natural tendencies and outlook on life. Rose-lovers are recognised as romantic and sensitive souls, while admirers of sunflowers are more likely to be outgoing and lively.

We hold flowers in such esteem that many people name their children after a flower. This name will hold personal and symbolic meaning for the parents and often they unconsciously hope that their offspring will develop similar charms and characteristics.

These preferences are an outer expression of our inner selves, so that when we are surrounded by these flowers we feel contented and relaxed. Our long-term attractions to flower families will indicate our general personality type. Some flower families have an out-going nature while others are more quiet and introverted.

Like people, the thousands of individual flowers that belong to the general group each have their own special characteristics which are peculiar to them. Each type of flower has a definite character; marjoram is warm and friendly, narcissus is mesmerising: a narcotic.

Flower emblems of the world

Flowers not only reflect our individual personality, they can also mirror the psyche of a nation. For thousands of years we have recognised that our national character traits can be symbolised by a flower or plant. We use these emblems to summon up national pride and make us feel good about ourselves. These flowers become a living testament to which we can strive as individuals and as a group.

The English rose is the symbol of love, beauty and perfection. We often describe a woman as being an English rose to suggest softness and sensitivity but this flower also reflects another side. Although the rose radiates beauty, it is also resilient and able to defend itself and even inflict wounds. Traditionally, the English rose would have been a wild rose, suggesting a person with a natural radiance. Today most people think of a hybrid tea-rose which has a voluptuous beauty but is also less hardy. Perhaps the English nation has become this type of rose, too.

The thistle is the flower emblem of Scotland. This beautiful flower symbolises independence and the ability to thrive in harsh conditions. Its healing properties strengthen the entire body and protect against physical illness. Certainly over the last few years, this spirit of independence has come to the fore with the new Scottish parliament and the determination to cure the ills of the past.

The Welsh daffodil is traditionally a singularly bright and trumpet-shaped flower. Its colour reflects confidence and power while its shape suggests communication through self-expression. Certainly music and song have been the traditional medium of expression for the Welsh people, enabling them to assert themselves as a nation.

The three-leafed shamrock or trefoil has been the Irish national emblem for over a thousand years. It is associated with the patron Saint of Ireland, St Patrick and the Holy Trinity. Its three leaves symbolise the bringing together of the body, mind and spirit. Ireland is in the process of bringing together its spiritual traditions with a new dynamic attitude and lifestyle.

The Dutch tulip can be seen as a flower of upright habit and its cup shape makes it a receptacle for receiving information and knowledge. These characteristics can be seen in the individuality and open-mindedness of this nation.

The lotus flower has long been associated with Ancient Egypt and India. Its many petals symbolised the mystical centre of life and its sudden appearance suggested new life. This flower certainly reflects a nation with a spiritual outlook at its heart.

The French have always been regarded as a nation of 'lovers'. Their sensual nature and love of food and wine is reflected in the fleur-de-lis. This flower also has a symmetrical and formal quality, revealing a nation which also likes refinement and the arts.

The poppy is the national state flower of California. This brightly coloured, orange-yellow flower reflects a sun-loving people full of vitality and energy. It also suggests a nation which is attracted to physical glitter and external show.

The tropical hibiscus flower hangs luxuriantly off deep-green foliage. This is the flower adopted by the Hawaiians as their national flower. Like this island people, the shape and red colouring of the flower suggests a loving people who enjoy the sensual and physical world.

In South Africa, the extraordinary flower of the protea expresses a nation that has a protective hard exterior, but one which has been regenerated by fire. The Australian acacia tree bears beautiful pale-cream sweet-smelling flowers. This sunshine flower of the wattle tree, reflects a nation that has struggled to survive in harsh conditions but through determination and optimism has forged ahead.

Japan has always been associated with its traditional flower, the cherry blossom. This fragile and short-lived flower is both delicate but prolific and symbolises abundance and friendship. The cherry tree itself symbolises hard work. The mass of flowers on the branches reflects a nation whose people know they have to work and live together in a confined space, so it is essential to get along with one another.

By planting the national flower in public places, nations can reflect on themselves, bringing pride, joy and upliftment to the souls of their people.

Inter-species communication

Flowers do not confine their healing properties to the human race, for they have healing properties for all the kingdoms as well as the earth itself. White flowers in spring cleanse and purify the earth, clearing away the decay of winter, while insects, birds and animals rely on flowers as food to keep them healthy. While this floral service is genetically programmed, some of the higher evolved plants – notably the orchids – have forged individual alliances with certain insects, birds and animals.

Just as humans are able to communicate with some more highly evolved animal species, so too can plants communicate with other kingdoms. They use a common language of shape, aroma and colour to convey messages to each other.

We can communicate with plants too, through using our 'inner senses' and higher mind. We need to connect to the spirit of the plant (or 'Deva'), which can be viewed as the 'higher mind' of the plant. On this level we share the universal mind, and can communicate freely. Understanding and using the language of flowers, helps us forge a new type of dialogue with the natural kingdom.

Flowers for self-reflection

Our appreciation of flowers is so unconscious and universal that we only ever allow ourselves a few moments to consciously savour their form, colour and beauty. This usually happens when we are walking in a garden or past a bowl of cut flowers. There is, however, another way of looking at nature and flowers, a way which is more than appreciation of their external form.

Disease has been described by English physician, Dr Edward Bach (1886 - 1936) in his treatise *Heal Thyself*, as a conflict between the personality and higher self, the soul. In order to be healthy and happy the different parts of our being need to be in harmony. Dr Bach's pioneering work was based on his belief that disease was preventable before its physical symptoms manifested. He created a series of 38 preparations from wild flowers and plants by transferring their healing vibrations to water through a method of solarisation. These preparations were found to be highly effective remedies for relieving the elements of discord within our personality before they developed into physical illness.

Plants can be viewed as a microcosm – a reflection of the outside world. For every person there is a flower that will reflect his or her life. The principle of like attracts like has been used for centuries and is termed the 'doctrine of signatures'. Dr Bach, who was a great exponent of this theory, developed the idea that we will naturally become attracted to a flower that mirrors a discordant state of mind. This flower also contains the energy pattern we require in order to regain harmony between the ego and soul. The plant kingdom acts as a bridge between the macrocosm and the microcosm – so, it mirrors the laws inherent in both.

Flowers are spun from light and contain electrical and magnetic vibrations. These act as a prism that reflects healing rays of light into our system as well as connecting us to universal forces. We can therefore use a flower to mirror our state of being and at the same use its healing power to correct any imbalances we find.

The flower is the part of the plant which talks the most intimately to us. The soul of the plant is not hidden inside it as the inner soul of humankind, it is projected through its colour, shape and aroma. So, when we look at a flower it is the external expression of our inner life.

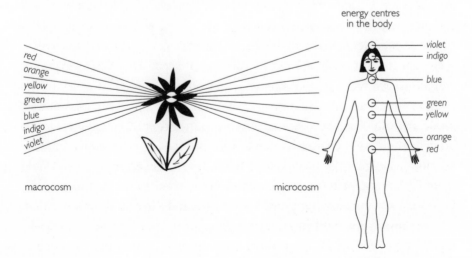

energy centres
in the body

red
orange
yellow
green
blue
indigo
violet

violet
indigo

blue

green
yellow

orange
red

macrocosm   microcosm

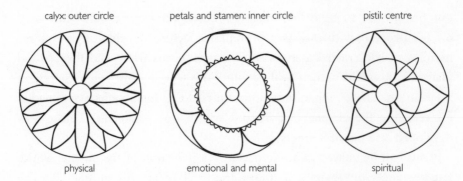

calyx: outer circle   petals and stamen: inner circle   pistil: centre

physical   emotional and mental   spiritual

Different parts of the flower mirror different parts of our being. So when looking at a flower from above, the outer circle will correspond to our physical body, the inner circle will correspond to our emotional and mental bodies, while the centre relates to our inner core or 'soul'.

All follow the same prototype although there are thousands of variations. When you look directly into the centre of most flowers it will have a centre core, inner ring of stamens and petals and outer ring of petals and sepals.

How your flower reflection can heal your life

Flower readings work on the idea that the shape, habitat and environment of the plant not only reflects our state of mind, but also provides information about our environmental and social situation which may be causing us stress. The person is seen holistically not only as an individual, but also as a social being interacting with their whole environment. Through the flower we can come to understand ourselves better and see our life in a clear and detached way. By bringing the unconscious to the conscious level we can empower ourselves to instigate changes which will create health and wholeness.

We can do this with the aid of the flower itself. The electro-magnetic vibrations held within each flower contain a positive blue-print which brings negative patterns into alignment. The resulting shift of consciousness accelerates the healing process. Further transformative qualities can be brought about by the flower's relationship with insects, birds and animals. If the flower has recently been visited by an insect, for example, it will hold these vibrational patterns which can be transferred to us. In this way the flower can also enhance our powers of internal and external communication.

Plants absorb and hold vibrational energy direct from sunlight. This is why mystics have referred to the spiritual forces in flowers as beings or angels of light. This radiant energy is converted by the plant into food for its growth and into a form that can be easily absorbed by insects and animals. The 'Deva' within the plant is responsible, along with the creator, for human existence and continued growth.

As the plant evolves and grows, its uppermost tips go through a wonderful metamorphosis and take on the shape of flowers. Unlike other parts of the plant, the flower holds and radiates outwards, vibrational energy. The shapes, colours and scents of the flowers hold vibrational information about the lessons and challenges of that plant essential for the plant's survival. If the flower is the mirror of our soul, we will also have to learn the same lessons and face similar challenges.

Not only do flowers convey messages to pollinating insects and birds, they hold messages regarding their healing potential in their shape, colour, form and pattern. Flowers are essential for our own survival too, as flowering plants make up over 80 per cent of all plant life on earth. If the flower kingdom does not survive, there is little hope for us.

The human being is also composed of a mass of moving energy particles of light, sound and electrical energy so it is not surprising that we are attracted to the flowers whose vibrational energy is similar to our own. This theory supposes that the creator has provided guidance for humans looking for remedies for their ills by imprinting on herbs and flowers certain outward signs which mimic the organ or illness that it could heal – for example the lungwort resembled the lungs, while walnuts looked like the two halves of the brain. The idea that like attracts like was used as far back as the German physician, Paracelcus, born in 1493 during the Middle Ages. This principle is now well established in homoeopathy and other areas of complementary medicine. There is, however, a more immediate and personal way of using flowers to reveal our deep-seated imbalances.

If we are experiencing problems in our life, we will be attracted to flowers whose vibrational energy we need. In fact, a flower will accurately mirror our physical and emotional state. These unconscious patterns, when revealed, empower us to make changes in our lives so that healing can take place. In the words of William Wordsworth (1770–1850):

> '*Thanks to the human heart by which we live,*
> *Thanks to the tenderness, its joys and fears.*
> *To me the meanest flower that blows can give*
> *Thoughts that do often lie too deep for tears.*'

The flower itself provides the healing blue-print we require to establish energetic harmony. When our internal vibrations are harmonious and the various parts of our being are in balance we experience good physical health and vitality, enjoy giving and receiving love and lead a full and happy life. The flowers we are attracted to will uplift us and help us achieve a feeling of peace and contentment.

Energy medicine

Over the last hundred years we have developed highly complex forms of medicine, which have, of necessity, made healing impersonal and have treated individual physical or emotional symptoms. If, however, we do not view ourselves as being separate from our environment, this has immense significance for the way we view and treat illness.

All life is inter-dependent and vital life-force energy flows through us connecting us to other life forms and cosmic forces. Our state of health at all levels is dependent on the quality and flow of energy between us and our surroundings. If energy flow is blocked, either in our body or from the universal flow, this throws our primary metabolic processes out of balance, while our ability to endure environmental stress is dramatically lowered.

Nature provides us with all our needs – food, water, shelter, clothing and fuel – and yet we are steadily cutting ourselves off from this primary source of sustenance. It is therefore essential for our own survival and that of the planet that we restore our respect and humility for plants. Much of our knowledge of plants and their flowers has been lost, but in an increasingly complex and stressful world we need to return to nature to provide a simple solution to restore inner and outer harmony.

Energy medicine is one of the oldest and purest forms of healing known to us. It is entirely safe and gentle and for this reason is used successfully on young and old alike. Medicine made from physical matter can only relate to the physical body as its vibrations are too coarse to penetrate to deeper levels of our energy system. There is an urgent need for a different type of medicine that addresses the more subtle parts of our being – dissolving stress at a deep level.

Different types of electro-magnetic vibrations of light, sound, aroma, and magnetic energy are the building blocks of energy medicine. These fine vibrations address the psychosomatic causes of disease, dissolving energy imbalances before they develop into physical symptoms. Electro-magnetic vibrations can be applied directly on the body by a trained therapist or through the simple medium of flower remedies which contain all these basic energy patterns.

The energy centres of the body

Each of us not only has a dense physical body, but also different bodies of consciousness, which support our emotional, mental and spiritual life. The energy in these bodies vibrates at a quicker pace making them invisible to the human eye and this is why they are often referred to as 'subtle' bodies. Uniquely, the mind can travel between these different levels. On the one hand, the mind is concerned with processing data in order for our body to function well, but on the other hand it is involved in activities associated with the spirit. The flow of cosmic energy through our physical and subtle bodies is essential for maintaining a healthy life.

Many ancient cultures speak of the power points in the body through which this vital life-giving energy flows. The Hopi Indians of North America viewed the human body as being built in accordance to the same principles of the earth. Both have a North/South axis which corresponds to the spinal cord. At one end, the brain is linked to the magnetic north, whereas the base of the spine is linked to the magnetic South. The spine is responsible, therefore, for maintaining a flow of vital energy and keeping balance in the body. All the internal organs and glands can be accessed from points along the spine, commonly referred to as *chakras*, and it is through these regulation points that the mind and physical functions can be brought into harmony.

As our emotional, mental and spiritual planes are interconnected, the chakras are the transformers or exchange points, which control energy from these higher frequency energy bodies. Cosmic energy flows through the spine, energising the chakras. Energy passes through the chakra centres and enters the physical body through the endocrine glands. These glands regulate all physical and emotional processes.

As the vital energy passes between each layer of our consciousness, it changes its rate of vibration in keeping with the pattern of vibration in that body. This is much the same as a radio with different stations tuned to different frequencies. The physical body can be likened to a station which is tuned to a long wave, while the emotional and mental body is tuned to medium wave, and the spiritual body is set to receive a short wave.

Flowers send out their own signals which are in tune with different levels of consciousness. These vibrations can permeate and change the frequency of our subtle bodies, according to aspects of our being with which they have an affinity. So the vibrations of different flowers will travel to the associated chakra and help restore balance of energy in that centre. Each chakra is connected to specific human qualities and life-themes. In India, the chakras were associated with certain colours, elements, symbols and properties. These relationships were written down in the ancient book of knowledge – the Vedas. When disease or illness developed it was believed that this was a result of energy imbalances within the subtle bodies. These correspondences were used to harmonise energy through the chakra system. By meditating on the related colour and sound, and visualising each chakra as a flower with a specific number of petals, the flow of harmonious energy could be restored. When our attention is focused on a particular chakra, we will be dealing with the theme associated with that energy centre. We can use flowers to help us identify the chakra centre and area of our life which requires our attention.

The beneficial effects and changes elicited by introducing real flowers and flower essences into the auric field can be clearly seen using a new technique of aura photography. This technique enables us to capture and view energy fields which surround living organisms. Now many complementary health practitioners are using these photos to identify where imbalances lie, and prove that shifts in energy have occurred after treatment.

Flower essence therapy

In the new millennium it is expected there will be a shift in the needs and levels of consciousness around the world. People feel let down by the so-called 'wonder drugs' which are proving ineffective against many virulent diseases and which cause distressing side effects. So many people will look towards preventative healthcare and natural forms of healing.

Disease rarely originates in the physical body, but has psychosomatic or psycho-spiritual causes. This means our state of mind and our emotions cause many diseases although we should never blame ourselves for our illness. Rather we should view our mind as an ally, which we can harness, as it has a major affect on our ability to heal. The mind-body connection is well proven, for every cell in our body is receptive to brain chemicals, and so our state of mind can affect the very core of our being.

Vibrational healing introduces harmonious vibrations into the system so that balance and harmony can be restored, much the same way as tuning a radio set.

Positive mental and emotional energy affects both the physical body and the subtle body, restoring harmony at a deeper level and at the source of the problem. In this way many ailments can be prevented before they manifest in the physical body.

Dr Bach's revolutionary realisation was that the colours, scent, and shape of a flower all combine to send out a very powerful magnetic frequency. This healing vibration can be captured in water without losing this elemental life-energy because water is an excellent conductor of electro-magnetic currents. The end result is a flower essence, which retains the healing frequency of the flower. So flower essences make use of the power of sunlight, and return the rays to us in a form we can utilise.

Flower essences have been called 'liquid consciousness' as they stimulate our consciousness and the capacity for self-reflection. They contain vibrational patterns of light, aroma and magnetic earth energy which act on all parts of our being. The patterns contained in flower and other environmental essences restore order and balance within our subtle bodies which, in turn, accelerate our inner healing mechanisms. Essences contain no physical plant material, but utilise the sun's rays to transfer the energy patterns of a flower into a receptive medium of water.

Back to basics

There is an explosion in the manufacture of flower, gem and environmental essences world-wide. The growth of flower and environmental essences is happening so quickly that their use is becoming increasingly complicated and difficult to control. There are now thousands of flower essences available and it is virtually impossible to study every flower in depth.

I think it is time that we look to the plant kingdom itself for the answers. We need to find and create a simple set of tools that can be applied directly and effectively to any flower in the world. Being able to understand and give flower readings is therefore not only helpful for personal development and growth, but also to the therapist who needs to find an appropriate flower essence quickly and efficiently.

Healing with flowers

When walking in a garden we are instinctively attracted to particular flowers, their shape, aroma and colour appealing to us depending on the way we feel at the time. Not only can you use your favourite flower to identify aspects within you that are out of balance, you can also use it to instigate a healing pattern in order to bring back this aspect into alignment. The message and healing quality of flowers is one of clarity and innocence.

Every flower has healing properties and it is a matter of finding the right one. Although Dr Bach and modern flower essence manufacturers have identified certain flowers as benefiting people suffering from a similar state of mind, this in effect is treating everyone suffering from the same symptoms with the same medicine. It takes a very skilled practitioner indeed to identify just the right combination of essences for the individual.

As multi-dimensional beings the energy within us is in a constant state of flux, and we need healing vibrations at a particular time that are unique to us. In other words, we need to find the flower with the specific vibrational pattern we need at the time. It is only through tuning in to our own vibrations that we can know our needs at any particular time.

Just as we have to feed ourselves, we also have to take responsibility for our own emotional and spiritual nourishment. Although other people can guide us towards an overall balanced diet, it is difficult for them to identify a particular food we require at any given moment. This applies to our needs at other levels which are highly complex and never static.

In order to satisfy our physical hunger and exact nutritional requirements, ideally we should eat locally produced seasonal food which is 'alive' and which can provide the immediate physical and vibrational energy we need. There are also now available hundreds of natural remedies that address specific mental and emotional disorders.

Remedies and potions assume that we have already developed mental, emotional or physical disturbances within us that need correcting. While many natural therapies make use of physical medicines derived from flowers, there is an older and more direct way we can use the subtle vibrations of flowers for maintaining good health and a balanced life.

This is the art of flower psychometry. By taking time to look deep into a flower it can open up a whole new world. Flowers teach us gentleness of touch, they teach us how to see and waken our hearts.

PART 2

Finding your flower

Tuning in to the natural world

Contacting the Deva of the flower

Finding your flower using colour photographs and drawings

Decoding the energy patterns

Giving a flower reading

Understanding energy patterns in relation to your inner state

Flower families and their central themes

Habitat – a key to your present circumstances

How your flower mimics your body language

Shape – the key to your state of mind

The energy of number

Insect energy

Finding your flower

Finding and reading a flower is a wonderful process of discovery and healing. You will need to set aside a couple of hours so you can enjoy the experience fully. I recommend you find your flower before doing your reflection reading. In this way your choice will not be influenced by what you have read. At later times, when you wish to repeat the exercise, the reading will still remain accurate as long as you work intuitively and do not allow your conscious mind to intervene and make the selection for you.

In order to 'read' the message a flower has for you, you need to find a flower yourself. Under no circumstances should you allow another person to choose a flower for you, as this will contain their vibrations and they could be projecting their problems onto you! It is important that you find the right flower for you, and no-one but yourself should make this choice. Some people feel equally drawn to more than one flower, and if this happens to you, make a mental note of which flower you were attracted to first. The flowers are first read separately and then as a pair.

Finding a flower is a simple and enjoyable experience but to get an accurate reading you need to have a good selection of flowers from which to choose. This will depend on the time of year and what type of garden you have access too. Although wildflowers growing in their natural environment are ideal, I have found that flowers growing in the proximity of a place similar to where you live give an accurate reading.

Obviously the best time to do a flower reading is the late spring or summer when there is a large variety of flowers in bloom. It doesn't matter whether the flowers are cultivated or wild – you will always find the right flower for you. Most gardens have wild herbs and flowers which have seeded themselves and even in city streets and parks you will be surprised how many hidden flowers you can find. Most flowers can be picked, especially if they are plentiful. You should, however, not pick a protected wild flower, but rather do your reading *in situ* or later at home. To aid you with this it is a good idea to make a note of the place, colour, number of petals and any other information to help you interpret the messages your flower holds.

If you wish to do a flower reading in the middle of winter or if you have no garden at all, flower readings work very well if you buy a large bunch of seasonal flowers or use a number of colour illustrations of flowers.

To create your own indoor flower selection, it is a good idea to collect some gardening magazines or mail-order catalogues and cut out between 20 and 30 pictures of individual flowers of varying shapes and colours. Select pictures which contain both close-ups of the flowers themselves as well as those showing the flower on the plant in its natural setting.

Tuning in to the natural world

In my experience it is not you who will be finding the flower – rather the flower will be finding you. Flowers attract and reveal themselves in a very personal and private way. This is why it is essential to 'tune' in to nature, so you can become sensitive to the vibrations of the flower that is contacting you. Often people report discovering flowers hidden in walls or growing in driveways or pavements and they all have commented how they felt drawn to that spot by the flower itself. One lady set her heart on an iris in the middle of a pond, even though it was extremely difficult to reach!

As the art of psychometry is closely linked to our intuition you need to get into the right mood to tune into your unconscious mind, which is in harmony with the natural world. Choose a time when you are on your own and won't be disturbed. The early morning is a good time to do this, as this is when a garden is particularly peaceful and fresh. The late afternoon or early evening in summer is another time of day when the aroma is full and colour iridescent. It doesn't matter if you wish to find a flower at another time of day as long as you follow the following sequence:

The first thing you need to do is get in touch with your emotions and feelings. Sit quietly for a few minutes either before you go into the garden or if you are in a garden. Take a few deep breaths and focus on your breathing for a few minutes. This exercise relaxes the mind and helps you tune in to your inner self so that you become aware of how you are feeling at the time.

When you are ready go into the garden, or starting walking through the countryside, become aware of the beauty around you and let yourself wander wherever you feel like going. Look at the shapes, sounds, colours in the garden, ground and sky. Become aware of the natural signs of nature and energy of different plants and trees. To help you do this, focus your attention on the spaces between objects rather than the objects themselves. If you half shut your eyes you will take in the view using your peripheral vision which will let you see nature in a new way. After a few minutes you will start to understand the relationships plants, trees and natural objects have with one another.

Sometimes the branches of two trees will lean over and touch one another, as if in communion. At other times you will find a plant that wants to stand alone, away from the crowd. Some plants are hidden away, while others seek out the sun. Try not to think too much about what you see, just become an observer wandering through a paradise.

As you move around looking and feeling nature, become aware of a magnetic 'pull' in a specific direction. Sometimes this is a strong feeling while at other times it just feels right to go in a particular direction. Follow the path you have been attracted to until you find the place that has drawn you to it. Once you feel you are in the right place, tune in to the plants around you. You may wish to sit down and look for the source of the attracting energy. It may be a tree, bush or small plant, bearing a number of flowers or, on the other hand, it may be a small single bloom. If it is a large plant, use your eyes to examine it, or if it's small enough, pass your hand over the top, without touching it until your hand comes to rest on a particular flower. This is the right flower for you.

Contacting the Deva of the flower

There is an interchange of energy between all living things, so the spaces in-between the objects are just as important as the objects themselves. In music it is the silence between the notes which enhance the melody. The butterfly's wing is made up of thousands of overlapping scales which reflect the light. It is the spaces between these scales which reflect the colour – and these are more iridescent than the colours reflected off the scales themselves. So, looking at the spaces between things can give us a glimpse of inner colours and higher octaves of energy which cannot be seen with our ocular vision.

All objects absorb and hold energy, but some materials are better than others at transmitting vibrations. So the outward appearance of an object only tells us about one aspect of that thing. To understand it fully we need to understand its inner energy patterns. Flowers hold energy vibrations which are captured from sunlight and expressed through their shape, colour and aroma.

These are outward manifestations of the inner energy as revealed by the 'doctrine of signatures' but we can also call upon the Devic kingdom to help us understand the hidden messages and healing qualities of a flower. Every flower has a spirit or Deva which is the equivalent of the 'higher mind' of the plant. As all kingdoms on earth are united at an energetic level, it is by communicating through our own intuitive higher mind that we become one with the spirit of nature and the cosmos.

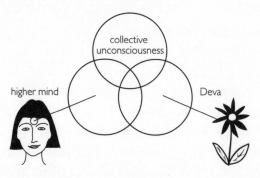

To start with, look closely at the plant and where it is growing. Perhaps it is in a clump of other plants, or maybe it has seeded itself next to a stone. Next, look at the shape of the flower and whether it hangs up or down, and whether it forms part of a cluster or grows alone. Try to distinguish the direction the energy is travelling through the flower. Stars and rounded shapes spread energy outwards, while lilies pull energy inwards. Bells often point to the ground, while upward pointed flowers direct energy skywards.

Look carefully at the colours and markings on the flower, as this way we can often find subtle changes of colour and texture which are not obvious at a first glance. Smell the flower and if it has a perfume become aware of how the aroma is affecting you. Once you have focused on the external attributes, it is time to go into the heart of the flower using your inner senses.

In order to fully understand your flower you need to examine it with your inner vision as well as your outer senses. The best way to do this is by doing a simple visualisation which opens your 'third eye' – the brow centre that enables us to see beyond the physical and enter inner places.

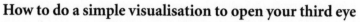

How to do a simple visualisation to open your third eye

Focus for a few moments on the centre of the flower and then close your eyes and take some deep slow breaths. Breathe slowly and rhythmically for a few minutes. Then concentrate on drawing your consciousness upwards to your third eye centre until you feel the whole force of your being located in this area. At this point it is a good idea to ask for help from the Deva or spirit of the flower. Ask that the Deva make themselves known to you through a colour, sound or symbol. Wait for this to happen. Sometimes you just get a feeling they are present and it is even possible to hear words or a voice of guidance. Tell the Deva to guide you so that you may understand the purpose of the flower and its special message for you. Journey into the centre of the flower and explore its inner beauty. During this time you may become aware of certain images, thoughts and feelings. When you intuitively feel the time is right, ask the Deva whether you can pick the flower and thank them for the knowledge they have given you. Open you eyes and let them rest softly on the flower for a few more minutes. If you have been guided to pick the flower, do so at this point. Pluck it gently making sure you make the break at the stem, so protecting the flower itself. This also provides you with a handle and you can return with it to do your flower reading in a suitable place.

✳ If you have found your flower you can move on to the section 'Giving a flower reading'.

Finding your flower using colour photographs and drawings

I have suggested you cut out a good selection of coloured photographs of flowers from magazines and catalogues. You will need at least 20 flowers to choose from, but a larger number will give you a more accurate reading. If you have found some unusual flowers, it is a good idea to leave their name tags for identification purposes. In this way you can also look up more about the flower's habitat in a reference book. As you may be influenced in your choice of pictures by your frame of mind and mood, make sure you collect the pictures over a few days or weeks. This will ensure you have a good variety of colours, shapes and types which do not relate specifically to your current mood. If this isn't possible, get someone else to help you with this task and you will have an enjoyable and interesting couple of hours.

Once you have made your collection of flower pictures, spread them out in front of you on a table top. A neutral background such as a white or beige tablecloth works best. When choosing a flower to read from pictures, it is better to select two flowers. The first will indicate your state of mind and present situation, while the second will give you guidance to the healing qualities you need.

Our eyes are our primary sensory organ and the stimuli we receive from the eye travel as impulses to the brain. Our brainwaves create energetic patterns related to our thoughts and feelings and we are often attracted to objects with similar vibrational energy to our own. The flower that we are visually attracted to will hold a sympathetic frequency revealed by its shape and growth pattern.

Your first choice, therefore, should be made using visual stimuli, and you can choose your flower by looking for the one that you feel the most attracted to at the time. Rather than just picking a flower straight away you need to tune in to your higher mind using the following breathing and visualisation technique. After you have done the visualisation with your eyes closed, open your eyes and, without trying to focus them, allow them to wander over the coloured pictures in front of you. Your eyes will naturally come to rest on the right flower.

When you have found your flower, remove it from the table. Now you are ready to find the second flower which has the healing energy you need in order to bring about transformation of any negative patterns.

Decoding the energy patterns

Once you have identified the energy pattern that reflects your own inner and outer situation, it is possible to find a new positive pattern to correct any imbalances you may have. Colour, texture and scent are the keys to healing energy, and although you will be able to see the colour of the flower from the picture, you will not be able to feel or smell its aroma. Again, it is a good idea to ask for help from the Deva of the flower you have just chosen.

Visualisation to help you select the right flower

Close your eyes and take a few deep breaths. Imagine a ball of white light above your head and every time you inhale, breathe in this light. Send it to all parts of your body. When you exhale, imagine your out breath as being dirty and brown. Breathe out all the negativity. Breathe in the white light again and breathe out the polluted energy again. Continue doing this, noticing how your exhaled breath becomes lighter and lighter until eventually you are breathing in and out white light. Once you have achieved this, call upon your inner guide and helper and ask them to make themselves known to you. They will give you a sign – perhaps a sound, colour, word or other symbol, or they may even take on the form of an angel, bird or animal. Once you have established contact with your helper, ask them for assistance in selecting the right flower for you. Thank them for their help. When you are ready open your eyes.

This is the time when our inner senses come into play, for we can select a flower not only with our eyes, but with our intuition. Close your eyes and pass your hand, with the palm open and downwards, over the pictures. Let your hand and intuition guide you. You may also like to focus on a problem you may be having or on the area of your life you wish to change. Move your hand over the pictures until it comes to rest over a flower. This is your healing flower.

* ✱ The first flower reveals your mental state and situation.
* ✱ The second flower holds the healing vibrational energy you need.

Giving a flower reading

In order to interpret the messages of your flower, you will need to look at it in several different ways as listed below. Each quality of your flower will reflect a different aspect of your life. It is a good idea to follow the same sequence each time you read a flower and make a note of the interpretations. By using your intuition and contacting the Deva of the flower you may also discover that the flower has a personal message for you. Once you have written down the significant points it is then possible to get a coherent overview of your present situation and indication of the healing potential which the flower can bring.

To make sure that you have not left out any important aspect of the flower reading, I have set out a form at the back of this book which you can photocopy and use for this purpose.

Flowers as symbols of our spiritual growth

Soul reflection

* ✳ Flower family – Central theme
* ✳ Habitat and growth pattern – Your present state of being and circumstances
* ✳ Shape of flower – Signifies any area of disharmony

Healing message and qualities of the flower

* ✳ Number of petals
* ✳ Colour
* ✳ Texture
* ✳ Aroma
* ✳ Insect, bird or animal energy

We will shortly go on to look at each of these topics in more detail.

Understanding energy patterns in relation to your inner state

When you have found your flower you can now begin to unravel its secrets. Read through this section and the next one on identifying the central theme. Then you can look for the section which relates to your flower in terms of shape, habitat, colour, texture, aroma and contact with other living kingdoms.

The basic structure of a flower when looking directly into its centre, reflects a model of our own energetic pattern. The inner most part of the flower, the ovary, represents the soul, for it is this receptive feminine energy that holds our full potential and links to the divine.

The stamens create a central ring around the ovary. These are highly sensitive, picking up vibrational signals from both outside and within. Theirs is a creative function which directs and channels energy into the centre. It is on the inner part of the petals that we often find a change of colour and other patterns and markings. This inner circle is similar to our soul which is surrounded by the energetic vibrations from our emotions and mind.

The success of the flower to reproduce is dependent on how well the flower is able to advertise and communicate its message and this is largely the function of the petals. If the flower is dependent on pollinating insects and birds the petals will be healthy, brightly coloured and scented. The petals therefore closely resemble our physical body which forms a protective sheath in which the finer parts of our being are housed. The most important qualities of the petals are their colour and texture as these reveal energy in our physical body and immediate environment. We use the petals to give us an indication of our present general state of health, social and economic circumstances.

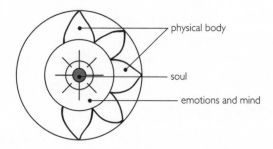

Flower families and their central themes

Unlike the wild countryside, we plan and control gardens so we can look upon the garden as a symbol of our conscious mind. By creating an enclosed sanctuary we are able to unravel the secrets of life for we can use flowers to help us bring the unconscious into the conscious in a loving and nurturing way. Wild flowers, on the other hand, represent the will of the Divine in nature and we are drawn to wild flowers at an unconscious level.

Each flower, whether it is wild or cultivated, has a central theme or key-note that reflects its main quality and purpose. The key-note of a flower is revealed by its most distinctive quality. It may be its shape, habit or colour and in some cases its known healing use or historical symbolic association.

The key-note of the hollyhock, for example, is apparent from its habit and texture. It is known as 'the flower of softness' for it is an attractive, mild plant which grows in fertile, damp places. Its leaves are velvety soft and its pink flowers are thin and papery. The blue spikes of the peppermint flower (*Mentha piperita*) have been used for centuries for cooking, medicines and perfumes. The wonderfully uplifting scent indicates a 'flower of refreshment'.

Other flowers like that of the yarrow (*Achillea millifolium*) takes its theme from its mythological and healing associations. Its folklore and religious associations acknowledge its astringent and anti-inflammatory properties and mystically it was used for psychic protection. So, yarrow is known as 'the flower of invulnerability'. The beautiful tropical flower the hibiscus (*H.rosa sinensis*) takes its theme from its scarlet red flower as this colour suggests a need for freeing up sensuality. It celebrates sexual expression and enjoyment.

Even if this theme is not immediately obvious, by contacting the Deva of the flower in the way described above, you will discover the central issue in your life at the present time.

Here are some common flower families and their central themes:

Rose family (*Rosaceae*) – love

Well-known flower families often share central issues. Perhaps the best-known family of flowers is the rose, universally associated with love and feminine beauty. The rose is linked with Venus, Aphrodite, Ishtar and Isis and historically became the symbol of virginity, martyrdom and love. Today the rose can teach us the lesson of learning through pain and love.

Roses have the botanical signature of five petals or multiples of five. This sacred number is closely linked to our own body, for we have five senses, five openings, and when outstretched our body creates a pentagram shape.

To find out more specifically the message the rose has for you, it is necessary to look at the habitat, and whether it is single, double, climbing, bush or spreading. A single-stemmed rose will herald one painful lesson, while a rambling rose will point towards many minor hurts throughout your life.

The colour will also indicate the type of love issue appropriate to you. Red relates to physical love, deep pink to unconditional love, pale pink to emotional and romantic love, white to pure love. A yellow rose suggests that you need to look at your views and beliefs about love, while peachy and apricot colours refer to an issue about communication and expression within love.

The rose family is not only confined to roses, but includes such plants as the cherry plum, blackthorn, hawthorn, crab apple, rowan (mountain ash), dog rose, wild strawberry and blackberry.

Iris family – inspiration

'Iris' comes from the Greek word for the eye of heaven which is usually associated with the rainbow. The iris is a symbol of purity and majesty and was the symbol of royalty since the days of Ancient Egypt. The pink flower symbolises holy love, while blue and violet flowers bring creative inspiration. All irises carry the message of communication between heaven and earth, so enable us to put our ideas into practice and raise our consciousness with divine upliftment.

Lily family – secrecy and feminine principle

Lilies are symbolic of purity and have always been linked to the feminine principle which brings the sacred feminine into the soul of both men and women. If you have chosen a lily it is likely the central theme for you is one of nurturing and feminine qualities of peace, calm and purity.

The tiger lily (*Lilium humboldtii*), with its orange and brown spots, suggests a tiger's markings, so its feminine strength is able to balance aggressive tendencies. Another lily which deals with sexuality is the Easter lily (*Lilium longiflorum*) (white) which helps you integrate sexuality with spirituality.

31

Bluebell family (*Endymion*) – confidence and security

Bluebells are found in the woods and gardens and grow happily under trees and in the shade. This reveals their key-note which is to enhance the ability to share happily with others. Their colouring contains cleansing vibrations that increase self-confidence and security.

Violet family (*Viola*) – thought and sensitivity

Violets and pansies are symbolic of thought and their five petals reflect the human body. They are linked to shyness and sensitivity. The lessons these flowers have as a central theme is learning to share of oneself without fear of criticism or failure. The healing vibrations of these flowers afford psychic shielding for those working as healers and mediums as well as psychological protection for those who have suffered trauma, shock or grief. Other flowers in this family are the dog violet, heartsease, fringed violet and sweet violet.

Snapdragon family (*Antirrhinum*) – courage and verbal communication

Snapdragons, as their name suggests, point at a nervousness and tendency to snap at people, often in self-defence. The central theme of this family is courage and self-confidence. The pink monkey-flower (*Mimulus lewisii*) reflects a fear of exposure and rejection by hiding your real feelings from others. The purple monkey-flower (*Mimulus kelloggii*) reflects a fear of rejection from a group, whether it is the family, peers or a religious community.

Daisy Family – innocence and survival

The common daisy (*Bellis perennis*) is recognised throughout the world for its cheerfulness and, because it is a favourite of children, is a symbol of innocence and survival. Chamomile (*Matricaria chamomilla*), and (*Bellis perennis Anthemis nobilis*), has daisy-like flowers. Its ability to grow in diverse and adverse conditions reveals a person who needs energy and patience in adversity or when they are in a hostile environment. The black-eyed Susan (*Tetratheca ericifolia*), however, looks at the darker or shadow side of the soul, which is indicated by its dark, ultra-violet coloured centre.

Snowdrop family (*Lily allium*) – life and hope

Snowdrops and daffodils belong to the same family. They inhabit damp woods, grasslands and gardens. Their flowers are bell- or trumpet-shaped and have been seen as a symbol of death, derived from the fact they appear to wear a shroud or burial robe. However, the snowdrop can also be seen as a symbol of life and hope since they are the first flowers to appear after the winter.

The daffodil is said to have been touched by Pluto and turned to gold from white. These bright flowers herald the coming of spring and in the Victorian language of flowers were believed to be the flower of regard. Their trumpet shapes suggest a theme of vocal celebration.

Orchid family (*Cypripedium*) – unity and co-operation

Orchids are dedicated to Venus, the goddess of love, and are ruled by her. They come in many different forms and colours but are the most highly evolved of all flowers. The shapes, colouring, scent and markings make orchids highly individual and the themes they convey are therefore extremely varied. The message the orchid family holds in common is its simplicity and grace, for several parts of the flower have merged with common purpose, so that this flower is able to lift consciousness through clarity of vision.

Lady's slipper is a beautiful wild orchid found in Europe, Asia and North America which resembles a shoe and grows in shady damp places in the woods. Its low-growing habit and dark red and cream colouring reflects a person who is suffering from sexual debility or nervous exhaustion. This orchid has four petals which link to the base chakra and so acts as a tonic and connects you with your inner resources of strength. Many tropical orchids have forged alliances with, and even exploit, animals and insects. They display intelligence beyond our expectations of the plant kingdom. Some orchids even mimic the markings, colouring and form of the insects they wish to attract.

Many wild orchids grow in pyramidal shapes, with flowers ascending up to a point. This enhances their transformative powers, especially when coloured mauve, pink or purple. Wild orchids with this theme include the early purple orchid found in woods and grasslands from April to June; the spotted orchid found in damp meadows and marshes from June to September and the bee orchid found in chalk and limestone banks. The fragrant orchid and pyramidal orchid can also be found in chalky grasslands during summer.

Parsley family (*Umbelliferae*) – balance and healing

The most distinctive quality about parsley is its rich green colour and feathery appearance. Most of the flowers in this family are delicate and white and seed themselves readily in gardens, fields, hedgerows and wastelands. Their central theme revolves around healing the heart. Their delicate appearance belies their inner strength and ability to adapt to many situations. This family includes many wild flowers such as chervil (cow parsley), water parsnip, hogweed, ground elder, wild carrot, and hedge parsley.

Foxglove family (*Scrophulariaceae*) – communication

The foxglove is steeped in magic and mystery and in Scotland is known as 'dead man's bells'. The foxglove, however, is not just associated with bad luck. As these flowers are a favourite with the bees, this indicates that they can be helpful in communication with the Devic and other kingdoms. The medicinal value of digitalis was known for thousands of years in Europe and North America, and in the 1900s the famous heart medicine, digoxin was produced from the plant. It is interesting that this remedy was made from the dark green leaves of digitalis, for in Colour Therapy the colour green is linked to the heart, which it benefits. The life theme of the foxglove, therefore, is communication with the heart. Other plants in this family include common speedwell, brooklime, mullein, eyebright, figwort and toadflax.

Here are some other flower families and their central themes:

* *Aloe family* – rejuvenation and energy

* *Arum family* – sexual conflicts

* *Allium family* – strength and resistance

* *Bellflower family* – bringing calmness into your life

* *Buttercup family* – self-esteem and inner worth

* *Camellia family* – celebration of your inner beauty

* *Conifers (catkins)* – self-acceptance and forgiveness

* *Currant* – developing hidden talents

* *Geranium family* – joy and creative expression

* *Jasmine* – innate femininity and wisdom

* *Heather family* – self-reliance and survival

* *Honeysuckle* – focus on the present

* *Grass family* – flexibility, commitment and finding focus

* *Eucalyptus* – purification

* *Marigold* – cycles of life

* *Mint* – mental or physical tiredness

✳ *Pea family* – faith and hope through emotional release

✳ *Pink family* – focus and clarity

✳ *Primrose* – lightness and cleansing

✳ *Poppy family* – courage to shine

✳ *Salvia family* – wisdom from experience

✳ *St. John's Wort* – courage, freedom and protection

✳ *Thyme family* – bravery and accelerated healing

✳ *Valerian family* – mental and physical stress

✳ *Waterlily family* (Nymphaea) – secrecy and shyness

✳ *Broadleaf trees* – (flowers of) balance and strength.

There are many other flower families that are peculiar to different parts of the world and that are too numerous to list here. To find their central theme and what they reflect in the human psyche, use the shape and colour sections that follow to identify their messages and healing properties.

Once you have identified the central issue that is important to you at this time, you can discover your present state of mind – both at a conscious and unconscious level. If you have more than one flower, it is the first flower you are attracted to that will act as a mirror of your soul energy and reveal your present circumstances.

Habitat – a key to your present circumstances

The place in which you find the flower growing is significant for its immediate environment will indicate your own personal situation. When we see the circumstances in which we find ourselves and our relationships to other people, we can understand that there are some things over which we have no control. By discovering how we are interacting with the world we learn acceptance but are also empowered to improve the quality of our life. By changing our attitudes and behaviour, we can influence the way other people view us and, as a result, we can improve our relationships with other people and the natural world.

Sun and shade

A plant growing in a sunny and fertile place indicates a person who is in a nurturing and creative environment, while a plant growing in a dry barren or windy position is similar to someone who finds themselves in less supportive circumstances. Some plants, however, grow healthily and strongly in very arid conditions and this reflects a person who is able to thrive in harsh physical or emotional conditions.

If your plant is growing under the shade of another, you may be afforded protection by a person who is stronger than you. It could also mean that you are overshadowed by someone close to you. If the plant is competing for light and air it would suggest you need to be more ambitious in your endeavours.

Single and double flowers

Flowers that grow singly are usually chosen by people who feel alone or wish to stand up for themselves, while flowers growing in a group or cluster reflect someone who needs group support. This may be from their family, friends or work colleagues. If the flower is one of a number, either on a bush or in a field, you may feel your special qualities are being hidden by others.

A large upright and robust flower suggests a physically strong person. If the flower is red, this refers to physical strength, if it is yellow it denotes mental strength and a bright pink or orange reflects emotional strength. Flowers of a bright violet indicate power and can reveal spiritual strength.

Small flowers

Small, delicate flowers reveal a sensitive and gentle soul. The place they grow in is important for often the smallest flower is the most beautiful and also often extremely hardy. Many people discover flowers growing in dry walls or cracks in buildings which seem to defy gravity and with no apparent nourishment. These flowers reflect a person who is often much more hardy than they appear, and they have wonderful resources of energy.

Hanging

The direction in which the flower grows is also important. Some flowers, like fuchsias (*Fuchsia hybrida*), hang downwards, their stamens pointing to the earth. These can reveal imbalances of mind which are repressed and held in, thus creating a number of physical and emotional problems. Generally, flowers that hang downwards appear earthbound and show a heaviness of heart. This means your life is being held back in some way and that you have a central issue related to 'embodiment' of your soul. Often people who choose these flowers have experienced a trauma early in life and are still holding on to the pain – which can become locked into the body tissue. You should not forget, however, that the flower also holds the key to unlocking this pain and turning the negative into positive through its healing vibrations.

Climbers

The key-note of climbing plants and vines relates to the direction you are taking in your life. You need to look at the movement of the climber and to see whether it is climbing in one direction or is spreading in many places at once. Often vines climb over other plants – in which case you could be using other people for support. On the other hand, some climbers and vines survive where others cannot. Some vines encircle other plants, binding them together, and their flowers will convey a theme of drawing different parts of your life together. It could also mean that you are a good mediator and can bring other people together.

Flowers that belong to this group include the sweet pea (*Lathyrus latifolius*) (red-purple) which helps you develop a spirit of community and finding a new home. The vine (*Vitus vinifera*) (green) balances the qualities of leadership with service. Honeysuckle (*Lonicara caprifolium*) (red-white) helps restore the feeling of being fully awake, especially where you may have had the tendency to live in the past.

How your flower mimics your body language

If we accept the universal law that 'like attracts like', we can use flowers to mirror our own state of being. It is likely we will be drawn to a flower that has similar qualities as ourselves.

Sometimes we are unable to verbalise our feelings and often we don't even know why we may be feeling irritable or upset. As flowers cannot speak verbally, they find other ways to communicate to us – making them an excellent tool to help us understand ourselves and deeper issues that we may not be confronting.

The most revealing way a plant can indicate to us how we are feeling is by mimicking our own body language. The way we sit and hold our heads is very similar to the way the plant grows and holds its flower. So, on a physical level, the shape of the flower often reflects our own body language and general personality. A flower may droop its head in despondency or it may express joy by following the sun with its petals wide open. A plant which bends and shakes in the breeze suggests a nervous person, while a tall upright stem may indicate someone who finds it difficult to let go.

Not only does the overall shape of the flower suggest our body language, it also indicates the emotional and mental state that underlies our physical demeanour. Dr Bach believed that the flower you are attracted to reveals your negative state of mind and, certainly, we can use the doctrine of signatures to discover any blocks we may have. I believe that the flowers reveal both positive and negative qualities and that they also show your current situation and state of being on all levels.

Shape – the key to your state of mind

We have discovered that the habitat and growth of a plant can tell us a great deal about our own inner and outer environment. From the flower family we can discover the aspect of our life that is central to our life at the moment. We now need to look more closely at the flower itself in order to discover the mental and emotional state that has developed due to the set of circumstances in which we find ourselves. So, if you have discovered that you are being over-shadowed by someone else who is stealing your light and air, it would be useful to know how you may have contributed to this situation and how it has affected your psyche.

Look at your flower, whether it is real or a picture, and decide which of the following shapes it most resembles. Then find the appropriate heading to discover what the flower reveals about your state of health.

* *Star*

* *Bell*

* *Cup*

* *Drooping sprays*

39

* *Radiating petals*

* *Cap or crescent*

* *Umbrels*

* *Pointed rods or whirls of flowers up a stem*

* *Trumpet shapes*

* *Candle or flame shaped*

* *Symbolic forms – wings, spines, tails.*

Star shapes

The purpose of many of the beautiful star-shaped flowers in the world is to remind us of our cosmic connections. These flowers usually have either five or six points, although some flowers create stars within stars by the radiating pattern of the anthers around the centre. All star shapes radiate energy outwards from the centre, so that our soul is lifted upwards towards the spirit. So if your flower is a star, this will have the effect of raising your consciousness and energy levels to another dimension. Flowers that reflect star shapes focus on different issues and provide special healing related to spiritual imbalances. Their key-notes and healing qualities will relate to the colours of the flowers. The following are some general characteristics but the specific shape of your chosen flower may suggest other imbalances to you.

Physical: A problem with nervous exhaustion and oversensitivity to your immediate environment

Emotional: Deep grief or inner trauma that needs to be released

Mental: Fears need to be dispelled so you can put issues into perspective and see your life more clearly

Spiritual: Your attention is focused on spiritual growth so you can follow your star

✳ Borage (blue) alleviates soul pain and a grieving heart.

✳ St John's Wort (yellow) is a provider of inner strength and protects against depression and fear.

✳ Star of Bethlehem (white) signifies inner peace to those who are severely traumatised.

✳ Iris (blue-violet) awakens the soul by inspiration and creativity.

✳ Star thistle (yellow) reflects a tendency to rigidity in outlook and a reclusive nature. Often people who choose this flower have the tendency to hoard material goods from fear or lack. The radiating yellow energy of the star thistle has a freeing action on the mind, and dispels your fears.

Bell shapes

These flowers enclose space and hang downwards, pointing to the earth. The imbalance therefore occurs as pain in the body, and as the soul struggles to accept confinement in the body. The individual who is drawn to a bell-shaped flower often needs grounding. These flowers can also help us turn our ideas, hopes and dreams into reality and release deep-seated blocks which are cutting us off from our vital energy.

Physical: Energy blocks that are draining your energy – these are often revealed in the need to collect, organise and arrange material objects

Emotional: Inability to express deep feelings and to return love

Mental: Mental blocks that have formed in childhood need to be broken

Spiritual: Guidance from within that needs to be grounded and put into practice in your life

✳ Fuchsias (*Fuchsia hybrida*) are very good examples of bell-shaped flowers. Their healing energy comes out of their centres which are often a different colouring from the outer tube-shaped sepals. This arrangement shows us that energy that has been hidden inside is being moved out and grounded. Often fuchsias are chosen when there is a body dysfunction as a result of deep emotional trauma and repression. So often our outer appearance hides a different state inside. This flower will help you release the associated feelings. The inner colour of the flower will indicate what sort of energy needs to be released. Red inner petals indicate release of sexual energy, pink removes repressed energy in the heart, purple or lilac ground the spirit, while white purifies the body and spirit.

* Fairy lantern (*Calochortus albus*) (white) indicates a state whereby you live in your dreams – which arrests your inner development and thus shows regressive tendencies. The white colour energy in this flower will purify you at soul level so you can reverse this tendency to move backwards.

* Bleeding heart (*Dicentra formosa*) (red). The key issue of this flower belongs, as its name suggests, to someone who harbours feelings of great attachment to others. The red energy of this flower gives you strength by kindling your inner fire so that you free your heart from bondage.

* Blue-bell (*Endymoin*) (blue). This flower reflects the need to slow down. It attracts a person who is stressed and needs to take a break. It also shows a person who needs regeneration, for the violet energy in bluebells purifies the woods after the decay of a long winter.

Cup shapes

Like a chalice, these flowers hold and receive soul forces. Their key-notes are nurturing and embracing and they show up imbalances in the emotional body where a person may be closed to their intuitive and feminine side. They may be suffering from a feeling of lack of support or rejection and need to experience love and close emotional contact to renew their faith in others.

Physical: Physical pain which has no apparent cause and can reflect emotional pain

Emotional: Learning to value yourself and increase self-worth so you can enjoy intimacy with others

Mental: Ability to communicate and receive guidance from the higher mind

Spiritual: Attraction to spiritual glitter, ritual, artificial highs, charismatic teachers and religious sects

* Evening primrose (*Oenothera biennis*) (yellow). These elegant tall plants with bright yellow cup-shaped flowers open at dusk so that night-flying insects such as moths can pollinate them. They symbolise hidden love and inconsistency in life as the flowers open and close. The softness of the petals and yellow colouring show someone who is gentle and sensitive and who may suffer from immune or nervous dysfunction.

* Star tulip (*Calochortus tolmiei*) (white/purple). These beautiful flowers indicate feminine receptivity and intuition.

* Californian poppy (*Eschscholzia*) (gold). These attractive glistening flowers show an attraction to spiritual glitter and glamour. Their golden ray helps you focus and bring wisdom into your life so you are not so easily deceived.

* *Protea repens.* The *Proteacea* family is indigenous to the Cape Peninsula in Southern Africa, although they also grow in other Mediterranean climates. The flowers are made up of numerous tough bracts which form a variety of open cup shapes. The stamens are often silky soft and form incredible spirals and other geometric patterns. The message of these flowers is one of physical strength and stamina in harsh conditions while maintaining a soft and receptive centre. The seeds of many proteas are only released by fire. Sometimes we, too, have to face a crisis before we can leave the past behind and leap forward.

Drooping sprays

These flowers grow on an arching branch, like a rainbow, and are often found on flowering shrubs. The flowers send out their energy in an arc or shower of light. The branches often sway and move about in the wind. An attraction to a spray of flowers can indicate that you require more physical flexibility, or it could be that you are holding onto rigid ideas and thought patterns. A drooping spray of flowers may also indicate a person who is easily swayed by others. The shape of flower reflects someone who has many hidden strengths and talents but who is weighed down by responsibility and narrow-mindedness. When they learn to relax and enjoy life they can get their message across to a great number of people.

Physical: Softness with strength is the key to good health and longevity

Emotional: Learning to go with the flow and not trying to control everything

Mental: Opening yourself up to new thoughts and ideas

Spiritual: Being centred and not chasing too many spiritual paths

Flowers which fall into this category include the following:

✳ Scotch broom (*Cytisus scoparius*) (yellow) brings optimism and a positive outlook when you feel weighed down by the world. It shows a need for positive caring and purpose in your life.

✳ The soft swaying and arching branches of the Willow (*Salix vitellina*) (green) indicate a flexibility and flowing of life. An attraction to the flower of the willow may show someone who is harbouring deep feelings of resentment and bitterness. They need to forgive and to accept the situation.

✳ Wisteria (*Wisteria sinensis*) (lilac). These gentle hanging sprays of flowers indicate someone who is afraid of intimacy and sexuality due to past experience. They need to release their fears.

✳ Quaking grass (*Briza maxima*) (green). Like many grasses which grow in a clump, Quaking grass represents someone who is finding difficulty balancing personal and group needs. It may also show difficulty in communicating in a group setting.

✳ Other flowers which hang in a spray are the silk tassel bush (*Garrya*), bush clover (*Lespedeza*), pheasant berry (*Leycesteria*) and sweetspire (*Itea*).

Radiating petals

These are round flowers with radiating petals which look like the sun and are often coloured red, orange, gold or yellow. They usually grow singly on a stem so are individual flowers which stand alone and which often attract bees. Attraction to these flowers suggests enhanced self-awareness and a need for solar strength. Often this person needs power by protection of light. The message these flowers hold revolves around the issues of self-confidence and empowerment.

Physical: To find inner strength to fight against illness and hardship

Emotional: A need to take back your personal power and allow joy into your life

Mental: Find expression for your individuality and creative ideas

Spiritual: Helps you tune in to the cycles of life and allows your inner radiance to shine out

✳ Echinacea (*Echinacea purpurea*) (pink/purple). This flower attracts people who find it difficult to balance their ego with humility – so, they find it difficult to give themselves credit where credit is due without feeling guilty.

✳ Sunflower (*Helianthus annuss*) (yellow). The great height of many sunflowers indicates a person who has strength of will and who may be arrogant or vain. It is also attractive to those who lack self-esteem and confidence. This flower helps you find your individuality and inner strength and fills you with solar radiance.

45

✳ Marigold (*Calendula officinalis*) (orange). These vibrant flowers are known as 'flowers of the sun' and their brightness suggests a need for warmth and nurturing. They encourage perceptive listening and communication within relationships.

✳ Zinnia (*Zinnia elegans*) (red). The bright stiff petals of the zinnia show a need to lighten up and not take yourself so seriously. Their sunny aspect will help you to laugh and enjoy yourself more.

✳ Cosmos (*Cosmos bipinnatus*) (red/purple/yellow). The delicate, feathery nature of the plant and flower shows a person who appears nervous in manner and speech. They are usually highly intelligent and need to learn to be more forceful in thinking and speaking.

✳ Chysanthemum (*C. morifolium*) (red/brown). The colour of these flowers shows attachment to the senses and lower mind as a means of feeling secure. There is often a hidden fear of death and this flower helps you to cultivate a spiritual identity.

✳ Daisy (*Bellis perennis*). Daisies pop up all over the place, like scattered ideas, so they are very attractive to tired, disorganised people. These flowers help you to integrate ideas into creative insight and meaning. Daisies also represent the inner child and innocence and it may be that you feel you have lost your spontaneity and ability to play if you are called by this flower.

Cap or crescent shapes

The crescent shape is linked to our throat energy centre and our powers of self-expression through the voice. Its significance is that of reminding you that you need to express your real feelings and talk about them in a non-confrontational situation. The cap shape is the crescent shape reversed and this shows you that you are capped or bottling something up.

Physical: Something in the area of the throat or neck is causing a bottling of energy

Emotional: Repressed emotions need releasing by talking or even singing, toning or humming

Mental: You need to release blocked energy in the mind so that you can move forward and reach your full potential

Spiritual: You need protection from too much advice and being swayed by other opinions. Tune in to your own intuition for guidance.

✳ Tiger lily (*Lilium tigrinum*). This is one of the oldest and most beautiful of flowers which often hangs its head so that the petals curl back like a Jester's hat. Its orange colouring relates strongly to the female reproduction system and emotions. Orange energy is a wonderful anti-depressant, and so the Jester's cap creates a feeling of fun and laughter. The spots which look like a tiger's markings suggest a flower which is good for feminine aggression, bringing a sense of calm within relationshiips and the ability to work co-operatively and in harmony with others.

✳ Nasturtium (*Tropaeolum majus*). The nasturtium is a bright annual which eagerly grows in even the most unfertile conditions. The intensely coloured flowers with a long spur look like fairy or elven caps, giving them a cheeky and cheerful personality. The flowers have a pungent smell and taste making this edible flower a good blood cleanser and an aid to elimination of toxins from the blood. The energy these flowers contain is warming and rejuvenating, and is especially attractive to those who feel mentally exhausted, or those who lack physical or emotional expression.

✳ Monk's hood (*Aconitum*) has flourished in British gardens for hundreds of years and all parts of the plant are poisonous. The hooded purple flowers are borne on tall spikes connected to the crown chakra in shape and colour. The lofty purple flowers have an air of spirituality and wisdom. This flower is good for anyone with difficulties which are rooted in the past and who needs psychic protection.

Umbels – many tiny flowers in a round or flat head

Flowers found in umbels spray outwards from the centre in an inverted triangle. They indicate integration of thoughts, ideas, and energies which need to be brought together into a balanced whole. A person choosing one of these flowers may be a healer or medium who is too open to psychic forces or someone who is extremely sensitive to the world and who needs protection. Often these flowers are coloured pale-pink or white, which indicates a connection to the spiritual realm.

Physical: Directing your energy to the important things in life so you are not exhausted

Emotional: Allowing you to value yourself more so you are not always trying to please others

Mental: Bringing together different ideas into an integrated whole

Spiritual: Spiritual focus and tuning in to the angelic realm

* Yarrow (*Achillea millefolium*) (white) encourages integrity and strength in those who are physically vulnerable and over-sensitive to negative influences.

* Pink yarrow (*Anchillea millefolium var. rubra*) (pink-purple) indicates a lack of emotional clarity, merging with others to please.

* Feverfew (*Tanacetum (Chrysanthemum) parthenium*) (white/yellow centre). These tiny daisy-like flowers indicate a need to bring your attention to other people rather than centring on yourself. They are often chosen by people who feel mentally restricted in some way or those who rely too heavily on logic and reason. This flower will help you to nurture your feminine side by caring for others and understanding others' needs.

* Angelica (*A. archangelica*) (white) connects you to unseen forces in the spiritual world, while receiving guidance and support on earth. This flowers shows you have a strong connection with the angelic realm.

* Red clover (*Trifolium pratense*) (magenta) is often attractive to those who need cleansing of the negative energy they have picked up from others. They may be responding to fear and panic around them and require calmness and clarity of vision.

* Garlic (*Allium sativum*). This orb of small flowers attracts people who are feeling weak and uncentred. They may be drained of energy and easily influenced by others. The ball of energy in the garlic flower imparts strength and resistance to outside influences by restoring wholeness of spirit.

Pointed rods and whirls of flowers up a stem

These are upright flowers growing on a spike and give the impression of pointing to the sky. This signature is usually related to the mind and spirit and indicates a person who is searching for upliftment and is a seeker after truth. These flowers are often chosen by people who drive themselves too hard and neglect their emotional and physical needs. They may also be prone to self-criticism. The healing properties bring upliftment and renew your energy levels, moving them upwards so you can accomplish your goals.

Physical: You need to be strong and protected against negative influences around you.

Emotional: Helping you learn from experience so you don't repeat negative emotional patterns

Mental: Finding your life's work and true path in life

Spiritual: Spiritual renewal, rejuvenation and psychic protection

* Lavender (*Lavendula officinalis*). This scented herb has been used for thousands of years for its medicinal and aromatic properties. Its upright shape and blue-violet colouring is associated with the head and crown chakra (energy centre). For this reason it is a perfect choice for someone who suffers from headaches, sore eyes or who has imbalances of the brain, central nervous system and spine. When you are feeling worn out or need to make a leap forward in your life, lavender uplifts and balances the psyche and draws our energy upwards to the spirit.

* Sage (*Salvia officinalis*). As the name suggests old age, the sage is associated with wisdom. It has an upright habit which relates to the

head and crown chakra. This shape enhances its capacity to draw wisdom from experience and this flower can help you find direction and purpose in life. Like many purple-coloured flowers, it has antiseptic and anti-bacterial healing properties which guard against infection and illness.

✳ Aloe (*Aloe vera*). This succulent of the lily family has upright, pointed flowers that are golden yellow and orange in colour. Their flame shape suggests renewal by fire and they are needed by people who are suffering from mental or physical burn-out. This flower can renew your will-power and physical strength so you can accomplish your goals.

✳ Peppermint (*Mentha piperita*) (pink-mauve). This aromatic herb has flowers that appear in whirls around the upright stem. These flowers suggest waves of rising energy, and peppermint has been known for centuries for its ability to improve mental alertness and agility. You will be attracted to this flower when you are feeling mentally dull and sluggish and your spirit needs refreshing and revitalising.

✳ Bottlebrush (*Callistemon Linearis*) (red). As the name suggests, these upright red flowers look like bottlebrushes. They will give you a thorough internal springclean especially when you are undergoing major life changes. This feeling of renewal and cleansing enables you to take on a new role with confidence and calmness.

Trumpet shapes

Flowers shaped like a trumpet reflect a theme of communication and self-expression. They teach the art of self-projection and give you confidence and the ability to express your feelings. Many flowers of this shape develop on vines and creepers, and the direction and growth of the plant can help you identify the area that will be most receptive to you. If the vine spreads in many directions, this will indicate to you that you should be spreading your message widely, while a flower on a single upright stem suggests you concentrate your efforts in one particular place. The colour of the trumpet will reflect the message. A yellow trumpet suggests expression of mental ideas, a pink flower heralds a message from the heart. White or violet are related to the spirit – perhaps you have a healing message.

Physical: The ability to speak in public and project your voice well

Emotional: Developing the ability to express your true feelings

Mental: Getting your ideas across and developing mental focus and clarity

Spiritual: Astral travelling through visualisation and inner projection

* Morning glory (*Ipomoea purpurea*) or bind-weed (blue). All flowers in the *Convulvulacea* family have a strong message with their five large petals united into a superb five-angled trumpet-shape, wide-open by day and rolled-up at night. Their colours include white, blue and purple. We must not forget that the plant is usually a climber or trailer and so the message of these trumpet flowers is spread over a wide area. Often their attraction results from feeling lethargic and foggy headed, especially in the morning. The vibrations of these flowers can awaken and refresh you.

* Trumpet vine (*Campsis tagliabuana*) (red). This flower dispels fear that others are judging you when you speak. It also brings vitality and liveliness into your speaking voice.

* Angel's trumpet (*Datura candida*) (white). This flower helps you to accept death and surrender to the spiritual process. Its trumpet shape signifies the angels heralding other worlds and helping us connect with these spiritual realms. The powerful scent, especially at night, links this flower to the mystery of the feminine principle.

* Daffodil (*Amaryllidaceae*). This golden flower heralds spring-time – a time for new ideas and plans. The symbolic meaning of this flower is regard, and a person attracted to its trumpet flower has an issue of regard to resolve. It also symbolises chivalry. The golden vibrations of this flower help communication, and increase creativity and optimism.

* Yerba santa (*Eriodyction glutinosum*). The flowers of this aromatic shrub are delicate blue and funnel-shaped. The blue colouring of the flowers relate to the throat chakra and, indeed, this herb is used as a remedy for colds, coughs and sore throats. The funnel shape indicates the ability to release the emotions, especially relating to grief and sadness buried in the heart. The blue energy restores the flow of natural feelings and so releases tightness in the chest.

✳ Narcissus (yellow/white) takes its name from the Greek myth. Narcissus was the son of Cephisus, the river god, and Liriope, a forest nymph. His beauty was such that he fell in love with his own reflection and eventually pined away and died at the edge of the water. Narcissus flowers grow by streams. Their golden crowns lean over as if seeking their reflection. The message of the narcissus is a paradox for you cannot love anyone while you are occupied with self-love, but you also need to value self before you can love another.

Candle or flame-shaped

The shape of a candle or flame suggests a flower with a strong link to the fire element. Fire has the ability to transform energy and is spiritually uplifting. A flower of this shape tells us that before we can move on we sometimes have to destroy and leave behind things we may be attached to and which are holding us back. The flame flower is able to cleanse and purify our mind and emotions, so that we feel renewed and regenerated.

Physical: Rejuvenation and physical purification

Emotional: Your old attachments must be severed in order for you to mature emotionally

Mental: Helps you adopt a new outlook on life

Spiritual: Spiritual upliftment and purity

✳ Mullein (*Verbascum thapsus*). This large flame-shaped rod of pale-yellow flowers is known as the 'flower of inner light'. The large, soft leaves feel woolly like a blanket and can afford you comfort and protection. The flowers, too, are renowned for their protective qualities against evil and illness.

✳ Red Hot Poker (*Kniphofia K. uvaria*) (orange/yellow). These flaming flowers are born on spiky foliage suggesting someone who desires to rise above the average person's expectations and social or economic standing. These flowers can help empower you to release your creative energy and ideas so that you can become an inspiration to others.

✳ Indian paintbrush (*Castilleja miniata*) (red) dispels lethargy and exhaustion and is especially attractive to people who need to stay grounded. This flower balances the physical forces in the body.

✳ Buddleia butterfly bush (white, pink, purple) is a vigorous shrub which bears a mass of sweet-smelling pyramid-shaped flowers which are particularly attractive to bees and butterflies. The shape and colouring of the flowers suggest a person who is in need of spiritual upliftment and cleansing. The strong link with the butterfly gives the Buddleia a strong transformative quality.

✳ Astilbe (*Astilbe*) (red/rose pink/white). This plant bears a large quantity of feathery plumes which point skywards. Although they are flame-shaped, their softness and pinky colours seems to quiver and suggest a flame of love situated in the heart. Their quality if one of abundance and a lifting of the heart and emotions.

Symbolic forms – wings, spines, tails

Flowers take on thousands of different forms, but perhaps the most beautiful and interesting are those which resemble winged or flying insects, or beings from other kingdoms such as witches or angels. In some places, flowers have been linked with fairies, elves, sprites and pixies. The foxglove was thought by the Ancient Britons to be the hiding-place of elves and fairies, while in Ireland the bells were thought of as fairy clothing – providing caps and petticoats. Sometimes the shapes and markings on a flower will suggest a face or even a whole body but these similarities are highly subjective and you need to tune in to the spirit of the flower in order to get precise information regarding these personal relationships.

Physical: Flowers which look as if they could fly, will lighten energy in the physical body

Emotional: Emotional blocks can be removed and literally fly away

Mental: Communication with other kingdoms can unlock meaningful insights and vision

Spiritual: These flowers link to your intuition and inner wisdom and afford you psychic protection

* Spider flower (*Cleome*) (white and pink). This unusual and exotic-looking flower grows on a large bushy plant. The scented flowers have long stamens which give the blooms a spidery appearance. Some people think that the flowers resemble a flying insect, in which case the pink colouring also links to movement and lightness of the heart.

* Slipper flower (*Calceolaria*) (yellow with red markings). These pouched flowers are extremely eye-catching. Their shape suggests a slipper and their colouring is linked strongly to the physical body. The message of these flowers rests with asking yourself whether you are taking the right step or decision regarding your path in life. Are you wearing your own or someone else's shoes?

* Honeysuckle (*Lonnicera caprifolium*) (creamy-white). The honeysuckle has traditionally been linked to a woman's love and lover's luck. Its binding habit and sweet-smelling flowers are extremely soporific and emotionally warming. The spidery flowers are a favourite of moths and so these flowers can link you to the powers of the night and mystical dreams.

* Chinese lantern (*Physalis*) (orange). The flowers of the Chinese lantern are small and white but often it is the papery lanterns that catch the eye. These are gold or flame-coloured and very appealing. The festive colouring and shape of the lanterns suggest a Chinese influence and you might discover a close connection with this part of the world. Some people who choose Chinese lanterns discover they have a Chinese spiritual guide or teacher.

* Columbine (*Aquilegia*) (white/purple). This is a very dainty flower often found in English cottage gardens. The petals form two five-pointed stars and it has four long spurs hanging behind its head. In the language of flowers the white columbine sent the message 'I was stupid to be so forward with you', while purple flowers showed resolve and that you would never give up. Some people see these flowers as fairy caps, for when you wear them you will be given inner sight and transported to other realms.

* Iris (*Iris versicolor*) (purple with white and yellow markings). This is a large group of flowers that are all extremely beautiful and varied in colouring. They have three inner petals that stand erect and three that hang downwards, creating a six-pointed star when viewed from

above. The name Iris is derived from the Greek word meaning a 'rainbow' which links the upper and lower realms. The flowers, too, look like angels which move between the physical and invisible spiritual worlds.

The energy of number

The spiritual significance of flowers is revealed in their forms by the number of petals they have. The growth and symmetry of the petals hold the cryptic keys to divine order and cosmic harmony. The greatest mathematical philosophers of ancient Babylonia and Greece and later India, believed that numbers could reveal the principles of creation and the laws of space and time. This is not such a far fetched idea because planetary rhythms are clearly discernable in the number of petals of flowers. If we trace the path of the planets in relation to the earth over a number of years, we discover that different planets create patterns of loops, whose numbers and structure are very similar to flower petals. In its cyclical path, Venus traces five loops which look like a beautiful five-petalled flower. The spiral arrangement of leaves up a stem is also revealed and closely resembles the growth pattern of the rose. The planet Mercury, on the other hand, traces a path of three inner and three outer loops, suggesting a floral pattern of three and six-petalled flowers such as those of the lily family, narcissus and iris.

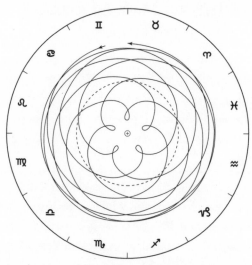

The rhythm of Venus
Movement of Venus around the earth every eight years reflects a five-petalled flower – a rose

Our own bodies too reflect these divine proportions. The planetary energy reflected by the number of petals in each flower has a direct relationship to our own energy patterns, and is linked closely to our chakra system. The energy from the different planetary forces regulates a different aspect of the world and therefore will also regulate the corresponding part of us.

The number of petals can be linked to various geometric shapes and these correspond to individual chakras within our etheric body.

When doing a flower reading, count the number of petals of your flower and discover which chakra centres are affected. Use the following table to discover which area of your being has the strongest connection with your flower. If your flower has too many petals to count use the 'thousand' petals analysis.

Numbers of petals and the aspects within us to which they relate

One **Heart**	This number links to the circle, and is the most perfect shape in the world. It builds an energy vortex of totality and wholeness and harmonises all systems in the body. An arum lily would be a good example of this. The white colour would signify purity and spirituality.
Two **Third eye**	Two petals often resemble a figure of eight which is a shape which harmonises with our third eye. This energy centre develops our inner vision and helps us see things more clearly. Many flowers only develop this two winged appearance when they have gone to seed.
Three **Body and mind and spirit**	The triangle has very powerful healing qualities and is linked to the number three and the bringing together of the body, mind and spirit. Flowers with three or two sets of three petals will amplify energy in your body so that healing can take place. It will also have healing and rejuvenation qualities.
Four **Base**	Four petals have long been associated with the energy centre at the base of our spine which is regarded as the seat of our will-power and life-force. A four-petalled flower helps you develop greater stability and equilibrium. It also amplifies and strengthens the life force energy in the base chakra.

Five **Solar-plexus**	Five is a pivotal number of movement and change. It represents the energy of the pentagon and five-pointed star. It provides a concentrated force of energy drawing healing angels of strength which are balancing and grounding.
Six **Heart and mind and spirit**	The energy of six links the heart and the mind, the lower with the higher, the divine with the spiritual. It brings all parts of us into alignment especially bringing our physical life into harmony with our spirit. It sets up an energy vibration that is strengthening and protecting.
Seven, 14, 21 **All parts of our being**	Seven is an extremely healing number which links to a seven-pointed star. It is a mystical number and this figure balances all the chakras, subtle bodies, and physiological systems of the body. It also invokes an energy which is the play of the seven major planets and is soothing to the emotions.
Eight **Masculine and feminine aspect** **Right and left brain**	The octagon or double cross is the symbol of rebirth and eternal life. It is represented by the number eight. Spatially, it is an emblem of cosmic equilibrium as it brings the four cardinal points together with four intermediate points which balance the four elements of earth, air, fire and water. It is a sign of new beginnings and stabilises the electro-magnetic field in the body. It also balances the left and right brain and the feminine and masculine aspect within us.
Nine **Mind and body and spirit**	This is linked to the Trinity as it is three times three so it is the triple synthesis of the body, mind and spirit. This number is therefore highly transformative and allows you to make a jump or leap forward with a sudden spark of divine knowledge.
Ten **Sacral and throat**	Ten is the number of completion and unity, for if you add the one and the zero you will get one. It is also the number of completion, helping you to reap the rewards from your efforts. It helps you to finish a task or relationship so you can move on without encumbrance.
Twelve **Heart**	The number twelve is the base number of space and time in ancient astronomy and astrology. It represents cosmic organisation into the hours of the day, calendar months and groups of years in China. It is the product of two powerful

	numbers, three and four, so is the union of the higher mind and spirit. A flower with twelve petals will help you develop the powers of empathy and compassion and link you to your intuition and feminine qualities.
Thousand **Crown and** *spirit*	This number is usually linked to the thousand-petalled lotus of enlightenment in yogic traditions. It symbolises spiritual growth and awakening. It is the divine and immortal soul that never dies. This number and flower will allow energy direct from the heart so you can give and receive unconditional love. It is the giver of life and resurrection so it brings a message of hope and eternal joy.

Insect energy

A wonderful mystery opens up when you study the relationship between the plant and the animal kingdom. The two are totally interwoven, and inter-dependent. All life forms are linked as the life-force energy flows through us at different frequencies. There is therefore no divine separation between plants or animals as they are all part of the same whole. Flowers rely on insects and animals for their survival, while the animal kingdom relies on plants for their sustenance. It is not merely the coming together of two separate kingdoms which is exciting but their magical dance where each step reflects the other.

Both plant and insect undergo a wonderful transformation in order to perform their special ritual of meeting. The plant must first develop a flower while the insect must develop through various stages of larvae and pupa before re-appearing in its resplendent finery as a fully fledged adult. The plant itself is made of segments in much the same way as the insect larvae, while the flower bud resembles the pupa, ready to unfurl and offer its gifts.

In the late 19th century, the scientific-spiritual researcher, Rudolph Steiner suggested that in previous ages of the earth's history, the plant and animal kingdoms were combined. We can still find flowers that mimic insects in markings, colourings and scent while others ensnare and eat insects in a way which is more like an animal predator than a flower. The petals of a flower resemble the mirror image of those of a butterfly or moth, while the anthers and stamens reach out as antennae which dance with the visiting pollinator.

Rudolph Steiner has this to say about the relationship between the flower and the butterfly: '*Look at any plant – it is the earthbound butterfly – it is the plant released by the Cosmos.*'

When applying this idea to flower readings, we should remember that the flower does not exist as a separate entity, in a vacuum. It is inextricably linked to the animal kingdom and therefore reflects our own connections with the universe and all living things. The energy within us creates a sympathetic vibration so that the physical form of the flower, the butterfly and our own body follows the same divine proportions and symmetry.

Sometimes while you are selecting your flower it will be visited by one of these insects. Its type, shape and colour, as well as the way it moves, will indicate the way your transformation will take place. Some insects are brightly coloured in order to warn off predators while others are well camouflaged by their markings. If your flower was visited by a contrasting coloured insect, it is likely you will become the centre of attraction but you may also make some enemies who feel threatened by the 'new' you. If the insect is difficult to see, the transformation may evolve almost unnoticed over a period of time. A grasshopper would indicate that changes will enable you to take a leap forward, while a slow-moving stick-insect will show you that slow and steady movement will be the best way to achieve your goals.

The large, brightly coloured sunflower with its radiating petals attracts honey-bees. The radiating self-confidence of the flower fills one with energy and the ability to create sweetness from one's work. The energy of the sunflower is not confined to the day, for at night it is also visited by lacewings, earwigs and grasshoppers. These creatures are able to move in different ways, showing you how you can deal with several projects at a time. If your flower had been visited by any of the following insects or animals, it will hold the vibrations and reflect the method of communication between them. By understanding the relationship between the flower and its visitor, you can be guided to the right action and changes you should make to improve your life.

* *Bee*   Hard work and diligence, paying attention to detail

* *Grasshopper*   Progress can be made in leaps and sudden revelations

* *Beetle*   Learning that everyone has a special gift – find yours

* *Ladybird*   Paying attention to natural signs and omens

✳ Snail	Relaxation and a steady, consistent path is required
✳ Butterfly	Allowing yourself freedom to fly and spread your wings
✳ Hoverfly	Taking time to investigate fully a particular thing
✳ Moth	Tuning in to your intuition and feminine aspect
✳ Dragonfly	Release through water and the emotions
✳ Wasp	Agility and quick-thinking, keep on your toes
✳ Spider	Networking and interweaving with other people
✳ Ant	Social and team-work, asking for help
✳ Fly	Versatility and the ability to see good in all things
✳ Hummingbird	Focus your energy in small concentrated bursts as this will bring rewards
✳ Cricket	Count your blessings and enjoy what you have
✳ Mantis	Bide your time, and choose the best place to be

If you are doing a flower reading using a bunch of picked flowers or flower cards, you can still connect to the insect and animal world. By doing this short visualisation you will discover the vibrational pattern of any insect or bird held by the flower you have chosen. You can also do this visualisation if you have a particular problem you wish to solve. Focus on the question you need answered for a few minutes.

When you have completed the visualisation it is a good idea to draw or write down your impressions. This will help you make sense of the things you have experienced and clarify any action you should be taking. Sometimes the message is not immediately apparent and the meaning takes time to emerge. In order to benefit from the vibrational energy captivated by your flower from other kingdoms, find a picture or other symbol or object that represents the insect in question and put this illustration in a prominent position in your home or by your work desk. This could be something like a 'spider' paperweight, or a dragonfly brooch.

Visualisation to detect insect or animal energy in a flower

Place the flower you have chosen in front of you on a table. Sit comfortably with your feet firmly on the ground and your hands resting on your knees. While looking at your flower, take some slow deep breaths. Blow out any stressful and negative energy you are holding. Do this a few times until you feel very relaxed. When you are ready, close your eyes and ask for the Deva or spirit of the flower to make themselves known to you. They may appear in the form of a sound, colour or feeling or even take a physical shape. Ask them whether your plant holds energy from another kingdom, and, if so, which insect or animal. Using your inner vision, visualise this creature visiting your flower. Watch how it moves, note its colouring and listen for any sounds it makes as all these things may be significant. You can also request for guidance and whether there is any special message for you – in particular, how you should go about solving a particular problem. Thank the Deva for their help and when you are ready open your eyes and let them rest again for a few minutes on the flower.

PART 3

The healing power of your flower

Transformative energy

Spirals

Flowers as mandalas

Colour

Texture – the key to the way healing takes place

Aroma

Preserving flower energy

Flower ceremonies

Flowers as meditation aids

Creating a healing essence from your flower

Taking flower essences

Healing themes of different flower essences of the world

Flowers linked to the five natural elements

Four case studies of flower readings

The healing power of your flower

By looking at the habit and shape of the flower you will have discovered your present state of mind and how this is affecting your life in general. We can now turn to the healing blue-print the flower contains in order to bring about positive changes so that you can work towards a happier and healthier future. These patterns are held in the colour, aroma and texture of the flower you have chosen. If you have two flowers, this positive energy will be revealed by your second choice.

Transformative energy

When Dr Bach described the process of discovering his flower remedies, he placed importance on the negative state of mind that was reflected by different flowers. Modern flower and environmental essence producers take a different approach. They focus on the transformative qualities of the flowers which act as a catalyst introducing positive energy patterns into our system, so that inner healing can take place.

Rather than being in conflict, these two approaches complement and enhance one another. All flowers reflect both negative and positive patterns and we are drawn to the healing energy we need due to imbalances in our system. The environment, habitat and growth of the plant acts as a mirror to our own life situation and environment, while the shape reflects messages from our emotional and mental body that may be influencing our physical well-being.

As the flower itself is the culmination of a wonderful transformative process, it also embodies finer vibrations that have developed as an expression of this evolution. Most plants start off green in colour, absorbing energy from the sun and water from the earth in order to power their growth. The plant's concern is the intake of energy into itself. It is only after it reaches maturity that it produces a flower, allowing the movement of energy to change direction which also changes its function. When comparing this to our own lives, we first have to come to know ourselves by looking inwards before we can really externalise our true thoughts and feelings. When we do this we improve our communication skills and relationships with other people.

The energy changes become apparent in the development of colouring and perfume in the flower. Both colour and aroma have their own inherent energy patterns that stimulate the release of energy from the flower. We can look on these vibrations as the heat which is applied to water thus agitating the molecules. This increase in movement allows transformation to take place so that the liquid is changed into a finer substance – steam. The movement of energy created by light and aroma also has the ability to move stagnant vibrations trapped in our energy system.

When the plant's energy radiates outwards from the flower it becomes the organ of communication. This transformation occurs because the plant needs to connect with other kingdoms in order to ensure its survival. Only the finer energy vibrations of colour and aroma are able to facilitate this communication.

When working with a particular flower, it will first facilitate an inward movement of energy so you come to understand your inner state. Once you have connected to your soul's energy, the impulses change direction and move outwards, so you can release deep-seated blocks and feelings that you may be harbouring. In this way, the flower acts both as your personal counsellor and healer.

Spirals

Spirals are seen in nature – from celestial galaxies to whirlwinds and whirlpools. In the animal world, too, spirals are found in serpents, conical shells and the human fingertips and hair. This mystical form is a dynamic symbol of the life-force and the rotating energy that drives the cosmos.

The movement of energy in flowers can be clearly seen in the wonderful spirals found in sunflowers, daisies, pine cones and thistles. In flowers the spiral is an open, flowing line that suggests extension, evolution and continuity. It creates a rhythm of life, like breathing itself.

The spiral pattern suggests a movement of energy outwards from the centre or soul of the flower. It indicates a time of great personal growth and upliftment, so if you have chosen a flower with a spiral you know that your inner energy is on an upward movement too. It may also show a longing for movement and change in your life, in which case you can use your flower as a mandala (which is a powerful meditation tool).

Flowers as mandalas

The mandala is one of the greatest sacred symbols embracing human experience. In India and Tibet, the word Mandala literally means 'circle' and this shape suggests universal perfection as well as perfection within us. The structure of a mandala can take many forms, but all mandalas incorporate a number of regular shapes and concentric rings leading the eye to a central point of focus. By concentrating on this form it acts as an aid to prayer and meditation, promoting a feeling of wholeness and at-oneness with the world.

Flowers are natural mandalas, some with beautiful arrangements of radiating petals surrounding a central point in the middle. By placing a flower on a table in front of you, you can use it as an aid to contemplation. Its symmetry and colouring can have a profound effect on your well-being.

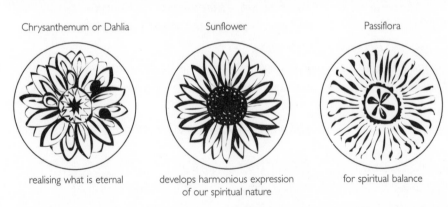

| Chrysanthemum or Dahlia | Sunflower | Passiflora |

realising what is eternal · develops harmonious expression of our spiritual nature · for spiritual balance

You can also use flowers as visual mandalas to represent the seven body energy centres – the chakras. Lie down, somewhere quiet, and place your flower on the chakra centre with which you think it has an affinity.

You will see that each chakra is strongly linked to the shapes, habitat and colours of flowers. The first chakra is linked to the earth element and colour red and the number four, so deep rooted flowers of this colour or number of petals will have the most pronounced effect on this area of your being and the related organs and body systems.

First Chakra:	**Base of the spine** 4/8 petals
Life Qualities:	basic needs and security, struggle for survival, assertive power
Glands and organs:	gonads, reproductive system, kidneys, bladder
Colour and element:	red/earth
Harmonious qualities:	vitality, activity, strength, sexual, stability
Disharmonious:	circulation and bladder problems, lethargy, sexual excess, lack of motivation or lack of will to live, unaware

Second Chakra:	**Sacral – pelvic area** 3/6 petals
Life Qualities:	feelings and emotions, sexuality, sensuality
Colour and element:	orange/water
Glands and organs:	spleen, blood and lymph, digestive juices, sexual fluids, tears
Harmonious qualities:	adaptability, self-satisfaction, good circulation
Disharmonious:	clumsiness, sexual problems, loneliness, relationship problems

Third Chakra:	**Solar-plexus – diaphragm** 5/10 petals
Life Qualities:	feelings and emotions, sexuality, sensuality
Colour and element:	yellow/fire
Glands and organs:	pancreas, gallbladder, liver, nervous system
Harmonious qualities:	courage, communication, independence, personal power
Disharmonious:	problems of the liver, gallbladder, jealousy, resentment

Fourth Chakra:	**Heart** 6/12 petals
Life Qualities:	healing, unconditional love, devotion, care
Colour and element:	green, white/air
Glands and organs:	thymus, heart, lungs, skin, blood, digestion
Harmonious qualities:	love, generosity, compassion, selflessness
Disharmonious:	breathing and circulation problems, heart problems, anxiety, indecision

Fifth Chakra:	**Throat** 8/16 petals
Life Qualities:	self-expression, communication, creativity
Colour and element:	light blue/air

Glands and organs:	thyroid, throat, neck, speech
Harmonious qualities:	expressing true feelings, creativity, good listener
Disharmonious:	anger, throat infections, poor communicator, cries easily

Sixth Chakra:	**Third Eye – brow** 2 petals
Life Qualities:	intuition, mental will-power, knowledge
Colour and element:	dark blue/ether
Glands and organs:	eyes, face, ears, lower brain, pituitary
Harmonious qualities:	intuition, high ideals, clarity, detachment from emotions, vision
Disharmonious:	dependence, unfulfilled desires, creative block

Seventh Chakra:	**Crown – top of the head** 1,000 petals
Life Qualities:	knowledge and enlightenment, spirituality, creativity
Colour and element:	space/ether
Glands and organs:	brain, central nervous system, pineal
Harmonious qualities:	peaceful and contentment, integrated life, enlightenment
Disharmonious:	fear of death, unconsciousness, coma, mental imbalance

Colour

Light in the form of colour energy provides every element necessary to maintain life on earth, and in order to be healthy we require a balance of all the rainbow colours. When we absorb a balance of the spectrum colours, harmony between the different facets of our being is maintained. Unfortunately there are many ways in which this balance becomes distorted. External factors such as air and noise pollution, strong emotions from other people and internal factors such as our own negative thoughts and feelings can create energy blocks that disturb this harmony.

Like pollinating insects and birds, when there is an energy imbalance in our system we seek out the colour energies we need to restore harmony. The light energy reflected by a flower contains the positive blue-print we require. The positive qualities the flower reveals are those qualities we need to work with and integrate into our system to restore balance in our life.

While the shape and habitat of a flower can help us identify an energy imbalance within us, it is the colour and scent that holds the key to its healing and transformative qualities. The plant uses colours and scent to attract pollinators – and the insects and birds respond to this colour energy, for the flower sustains their lives, too. Colour and aroma are therefore the tools whereby the plant communicates and forges a link with other kingdoms. In order for the plant to change a green leaf into a flower, it undergoes a wonderful transformation utilising the energy from sunlight. We can also instigate positive changes in our life by using the energetic information revealed by the colour of the flower.

Kirlian photography and aura imaging

The existence of a subtle energy field, often referred to as the 'aura', around living organisms has been known for thousands of years. Throughout history people with clairvoyant vision have reported seeing a mass of swirling colours surrounding individuals. Now modern scientific research in the form of aura imaging is verifying its reality. Recording the energy field started in earnest during the 1930s and 40s in Russia. The best known exponent of Kirlian photography was the Russian, Semycn Kirlian. He invented a camera which viewed the body through a special plate using ultra-violet light, with the result he could view and record the ethereal and electrical current around the subject.

From acupuncture and reflexology we know that many energy pathways run through the entire body, and that this vital energy accumulates at various points on the skin and end points of the meridians in the hands and feet. Kirlian photography was able to confirm this ancient Chinese knowledge.

Kirlian and aura photography reveals the differences between the intensity and range of colours in the aura when we are exposed to different colour wavelengths.

The Phantom leaf

Several researchers including Allen Detrick and I. Dumiytrescu, discovered that when they cut a leaf in half, the Kirlian photograph revealed the shape of the complete leaf around each of the separated halves. They concluded that each organism has an imprinted pattern of energy flow which is maintained even when part of the physical body is removed. Some theorists believe this can account for the 'phantom limb' phenomenon, where a person continues to feel the pain and even feelings associated with a lost limb. To vibrational healers, this makes perfect sense, for we believe that the human being is not only made up of the dense physical form, but other much more subtle bodies which vibrate at a higher frequency thus making them invisible to the naked eye.

The beneficial effects and changes elicited by introducing the energy of flowers and flower essences into the auric field can be clearly seen using aura photography, and now many practitioners are using these photos to identify where imbalances lie, and proof of shifts in energy after treatment.

Light and dark colours

Not only do we have a dense physical body, we also have several 'light' bodies which vibrate at a higher frequency, thus making them invisible to normal vision. Colour energy is a vibration which can permeate our aura and affect our subtle bodies and energy system. Through sympathetic resonance each colour vibration moves to the area where healing is needed. The colours in the aura will change when a flower is brought into our auric field. After the flower energy is introduced these hues become much clearer and brighter. Kirlian and aura photography reveal the differences between the intensity and range of colours in the aura when the colour vibration is picked up by our energy system.

The healing quality of the flower also depends on the intensity of the colour energy. The darker and more dense the colour, the more light energy is reflected away from the plant; the paler and more translucent the colour, the more light energy it contains. Darker tones have the strongest effect on our physical body, while pale colours have finer vibrations that are able to penetrate our subtle bodies. Some flowers have a combination of colour intensities – for example, bright, dark-coloured centres with translucent petals will work on more than one level simultaneously.

Clear, iridescent colours are extremely powerful and work through the astral and mental body, while softer lighter versions of the same colour will work on higher levels of consciousness through the spiritual bodies. A flower with several colours will be working at several levels, be it physical, emotional, mental or spiritual. When a plant has more than one colour signature, the different colour energy patterns released by the treatments will travel to different parts of our being.

Look at the colours of your flower and discover which levels of your being the vibrations will heal. The type of aroma will also indicate which of your bodies will have a sympathetic resonance.

Colours	Aroma	Level of healing
Dark colours	heavy, rich, woody	physical and etheric body
Bright and clear	refreshing, sweet	emotional and mental body
Light colours	light, euphoric	spiritual bodies

Life themes of the different colours

We have discovered that each flower family has a particular life quality or theme. This applies to colour families, too. Each group of colours from the darkest to the lightest tint shares the same essence as one of the rainbow colours. These life-giving solar vibrations have distinct healing qualities and can indicate the individual lessons we need to learn in order to grow and develop.

White and purple are both highly transformational vibrations which are linked to the spiritual worlds and the life theme of growth, maturation and ageing. A white, lilac, or purple flower indicates issues revolving around the child and parent relationships and finality of dying.

Blue flowers relate to the theme of helping you develop hope and trust, especially where you have lost faith in yourself and others. It is the colour that encourages feminine intuition and self-expression, so that you can vocalise your feelings in a non-aggressive way.

Green flowers are less common and are generally found on grasses and trees that rely on the elements of wind for pollination. If you choose a green flower, its shape, habitat and growth pattern will be most important in obtaining a true reading. Green balances the emotions, especially where you may be subject to mood swings. It links one to the natural world and natural rhythms, bringing flexibility of mind and harmony within the body.

Orange coloured flowers are universally regarded as bringers of joy and mental upliftment and, as a result, are wonderful anti-depressants. They encourage sociability and communication within relationships. The life theme of orange flowers is one of social integration.

Red flowers link strongly to the physical realm. Being the colour of blood, they relate to the primal fire and our basic life-force energy. Red is also the colour of physical love and procreation and their theme relates to will-power and the ability to walk purposefully along your chosen path.

Yellow flowers are strongly related to the ego and the lower mind. This area of our being governs all mental processes learned in childhood and reinforced during our lives. Yellow vibrations relate to language skills, memory, logic and analysis, so yellow flowers strengthen these aspects of the mind. They are also uplifting, centring and focusing, and golden-yellow opens up our receptivity to new ideas and helps us bring wisdom into our affairs. Yellow is also the colour vibration which has an affinity with our solar-plexus, the seat of our personal power. It helps build up our self-confidence and dispel our fears.

Black and ultra-violet are colours not readily found in nature. Although there is no true black, many flowers have blue-black markings that are really ultra-violet vibrations. This part of the spectrum is beyond our vision but can be revealed under ultra-violet light. Dark-violet colouring in flowers indicates the darker side often referred to as the 'shadow' self. Black flowers can help us bring the unconscious to the conscious, thus bringing the shadow into the light and bringing remarkable spiritual healing. When looking into a flower, the area of the ultra-violet marks will show you where the internal energy blocks lie (turn back to the energy diagram of a flower in Part 2, Understanding energy patterns, page 29).

Hidden agendas

Many flowers have hidden agendas, and when viewed under ultra-violet light reveal intricate arrangements and patterns that can only be seen by pollinating bees or insects. If you are collecting and making your own flower essences you will need to check whether the flower has a hidden ultra-violet message. Many people working with flowers and their devas identify these patterns using their intuition. For a novice, however, you need to tune in to the spirit of the flower using the visualisation described for picking your flower.

Texture – the key to the way healing takes place

The depth of colour of a flower often goes hand in hand with its texture. The texture of your chosen flower can help you identify the way in which the healing is going to work. Sometimes it is by providing you with a protective shield, while at other times you may need to make changes from within. When you know how the imbalances are to be corrected you will be able to choose appropriate ways of using the flower, colour and scent to speed up this process.

Thick glossy petals reflect the light and have a rich and shining appearance. These reflective rays help you radiate the qualities of the colour to all around you. In this way you can change other people's reactions and attitudes towards you, thus improving your relationships. Shiny flowers provide you with a cloak of protection by deflecting harmful energy away from you, allowing you to heal within. Your new glow of health and positive attitudes will be an example to others.

Some flowers have paper-thin petals that allow the light to penetrate. Often they are coloured in pastel and light shades which indicate that their healing energy is linked to transformation in the spiritual realm. These delicate flowers permeate your subtle bodies. Often the changes are imperceptible at first and sometimes take a long time to reach the physical dimension. The more sensitive you are to your intuition, the more able you will be to detect these subtle healing vibrations. You need to exercise patience, but change will come.

Clusters of small flowers often have a downy or cotton-wool appearance and feel. They are frothy and light to touch. Meadowsweet is soft and sweet-smelling, reflecting healing properties of nurturing and comforting. Their feather-like qualities allow us to relax and drift peacefully through difficult times. Eucalyptus flowers are also aromatic. The flowers form rosettes of thousands of creamy white stamens. The sweetness and sensitivity of both these flowers help us to still fears and anxieties so that we can build up our trust in the divine. The healing power of soft catkins comes from movement and flexibility, helping you introduce changes and face the unexpected.

Flowers that are stiff and waxy to the touch are often found on succulents and plants which live in dry, arid conditions. Their external strength and rigidity comes from their ability to hold water. Likewise, these flowers help you develop the stamina and physical strength to meet and overcome difficult challenges and hardships, while maintaining a sensitivity and compassionate outlook on the inside. The key to their healing quality lies in making sure you do not become critical and resentful.

Lavender flowers are quite firm but are silky to the touch, and there are many other flowers that are covered in fine silky hairs. Borage flowers are in themselves quite firm and waxy, but their sepals are edged with fine silver hairs. When the flowers open, these hairs radiate like stars. Here, the healing properties work on two levels which link in with the stellar shape. The purple flowers bring optimism and resilience and act as spiritual transmitters, while the silver and green bracts resemble antennae, picking up healing vibrations from the universe.

It is difficult to imagine a flower being hard to the touch, but there are some flowers that are protected by spiky thorns and bracts. The flower of the blessed thistle (*Cnicus benedictus*) has threatening points and is a symbol of independence and protection against negative influences.

Some apparently hard and spiky flowers are also covered with fine hair. The flower of the bulrush is upright and straight, but on closer inspection is covered with soft fine hair. The velvety covering feels similar to the coat of a mole, which when stroked can soften the most hardened heart.

Many grasses and rushes have flowers that feel and sound like parchment. Their papery flowers depend on wind for pollination and if you rub them gently in your hand they will give out healing sounds. If you listen carefully to their whispers they can enable you to tune in to the song of the universe and the divine word.

Aroma

One of the greatest gifts flowers give us is their aroma, for through it the flower achieves true alchemy by transforming earthbound energy into moveable ethereal vibrations. This metamorphosis of shape, colour and aroma transforms leaves into flowers, and petals into stamens as the plant must now reach out to the universe and spread a greater message. In this way the scent allows the flower to move, to fly.

When you drink in the aroma of the flower, its healing qualities are immediate. The vibrational energy travels directly to the limbic brain, the seat of our emotional memory. By linking a feeling of well-being and health to the perfume of your flower, this association is held within the brain and can be unlocked at a later date when triggered by a similar aroma. We respond to colour vibrations in the same way for these impulses travel to the limbic area creating an immediate emotional response. This is why we instinctively appreciate a beautiful sunset or rainbow without analysing what we see.

Unfortunately the beauty of the colour and aroma of a flower is transitory. However, although you will only be able to sniff the perfume of your flower just a few times, its healing work will continue long after your flower has withered. The fine aromatic vibrations activate stagnant energy in our emotional and mental body, thus restoring a free flow of life nurturing vibrations through our system. For a more long-term benefit you can also introduce similar scents into your life by using essential oils in cosmetics, bath essences, and floral waters as sprays and perfumes. The close relationship of colour and aroma allows us to use the colour of the flower as a substitute for healing when the aroma has faded. This is particularly useful if you are using a picture of a flower for your flower reading since you will not be able to smell its aroma.

In order to discover the colour that relates to the aroma of a flower we have to link types of aromatic notes to particular colour wave-lengths. To help us do this we have to create a scale of notes starting at the lowest or base notes and then progressing to the highest or top notes. Both colour and aroma vibrations can be linked to this scale.

Colours	*Aromas*
Long wave-lengths	Base notes
Middle wave-lengths	Middle notes
Short wave-lengths	Top notes

The aroma of a red-coloured flower corresponds to stimulating and energising aromas such as essential oil of ylang ylang, cedar or sandalwood or fresh ginger. Red and pink flowers are the colours of love that promote the flow of loving vibrations in your life. Pink flowers contain energy that balances the heart and the aroma of rose-water or oils made from rose, melissa or palmarosa will have a similar healing affect.

The scent of orange-coloured flowers can be restored with the use of orange-flower water, the smell of fresh peaches and apricots and the aroma of cooking spices such as cinnamon and cardamom.

Yellow flowers contain uplifting and empowering vibrations that work through the nervous system and stimulate mental functions. Aromas that have similar qualities include the scent of fresh grapefruit, lemon and lime. You can also make floral water by adding a few drops of the essential oils of these fruits into a plant spray of pure water.

Aromatic vibrations that link to the colour green contain harmonising and normalising qualities. They are relaxing to the mind and emotions and include the aroma of fresh lemon verbena or peppermint, rose-geranium leaves, rose-water, eucalyptus leaves and essential oil of bergamot.

The blue wave-length has sedative and cooling qualities and the aromas which harmonise with this colour are cloves, thyme, sandalwood, chamomile and marjoram.

Violet is a fine vibration that has spiritually uplifting qualities. Aromas of violets, lavender and rosemary encourage the same type of transformative healing qualities.

The aroma of white flowers cleanses and purifies the emotions and spirit. You can introduce these soothing vibrations with the aroma of jasmine, gardenia, lily of the valley or magnolia.

Preserving flower energy

When you have picked a flower for your reading it is possible to enjoy its beauty for a short time until it withers and dies. There are, however, several ways you can enjoy the healing energy from your flower for longer.

If you have picked a flower with a long-enough stem, it is possible to put your flower in a vase of water to which a couple of drops of Dr Bach's Rescue Remedy have been added. This remedy is specially formulated from five flowers which have been found to alleviate stress and shock in both plants and animals. Place your flower in a place where you can drink in its vibrations as often as possible. I usually keep a flower on my desk or dressing table and allow my eyes to rest on it every few minutes while I am sitting there. The colour vibrations and aroma will permeate your aura and shift your subtle bodies into alignment.

A flower that has no stem can be floated in a glass bowl on a table. A good place for these flowers is on a dining or coffee table. With the addition of floating candles which reflect light off the petals, your flower will make a perfect tool for contemplation and meditation. You could also add a few drops of harmonising essential oil or flower essence into the water. Concentrate on the area of your being that needs bringing into balance while allowing your eyes to rest unfocused on the floating flower. You can also contact the Deva of the flower while doing this exercise and ask for any specific help you may need in bringing about positive changes in your life.

Both the methods I have described above allow healing vibrations to enter your system immediately, but often the healing process is a slow one and the effect of the flower vibrations needs to be sustained over a longer period of time.

Flower ceremonies

Creating a flower ceremony is a powerful means of remembering the message your flower brings you. Such a ceremony is an ancient way of connecting with the cyclical nature of the divine forces and it gives us the opportunity to mindfully put back what we have taken out. The rhythmic movement of the ceremony connects us to life cycles and natural energy, for like life, it has a beginning, middle and end which is repeated at different times.

The ceremony allows you to focus on the lessons you have to learn and helps you create a balance between the positive and negative aspects within you. It requires you to make a personal commitment and dedication to improving your life and thus working towards a better world. The revelation of power and beauty of the ceremony depends on how you individually experience the process. If you approach the ceremony with humility and sincerity you will open yourself up to the divine so that you can receive the healing power of love.

The questions posed in the flower reflection reading are a good starting place for your own journey. Make a list of things you wish to create in your life and qualities you wish to develop. These may include things like hope, trust, love or abundance.

Check the number of petals on your flower and make sure you have written a quality that you wish to bring into your life for each petal. If you have a flower with one fused petal, choose the quality that is most important to you. Should your flower have too many petals to count, choose an appropriate number that will link to several petals at once.

For your flower ceremony you need:

* a clear glass bowl of natural or spring water

* two candles and matches

* absorbent paper towels

* an envelope

* your flower (try to have one with a stem)

* two twigs.

Beginning the ceremony

Create a small altar with a cloth on a table or the floor, making sure it is somewhere quiet. Half fill your glass bowl with water and put the two candles on either side. Take a few minutes to close your eyes and slow down your breathing so that it is regular and deep.

Mindfully, light the two candles. The first symbolises the physical body and the second the higher mind and spirit. Be aware that these two aspects are sustained by the same divine light.

Pick up your flower and begin by dedicating it to someone or something of your choosing. You may decide to dedicate your flower to your own inner healing, your family or loved ones, or a group of people or a place.

Hold your flower by the stem and gently pull off each petal and place it in the bowl of water. Each petal represents one of the qualities you wish to bring into your life. Concentrate and say aloud 'This petal represents…'.

When you have removed all the petals you will be left with the centre of the flower. This represents the central or combining force within you. Lay this part and the stem next to the bowl.

You can spend as long as you like looking at the petals floating on the water or meditating with your eyes shut. When you have finished, gently lift the petals out of the water with your twigs and place them on the absorbent paper towel. Leave them to dry. While you are waiting for them make another list. This time write down your grudges and resentments and any negative traits in yourself that you wish to change. Place this list in the envelope. Return to your petals when they are dry and place them in the envelope also. Seal the envelope.

Finale

Put the envelope with the petals and list under your bed or inside your pillow cover if you think it will not disturb your sleep. Leave it there overnight. Many people are able to recall vivid dreams when performing this ceremony while others say they sleep soundly with no recall at all. Whether you remember your dreams or not, shifts in the unconscious mind take place during deep sleep. This movement of energy works on a very subtle level, but can also be extremely powerful. Sometimes you will find that you are able to solve a problem or make a difficult decision very easily after this ceremony. At other times problems may take longer to resolve, but rest assured that you will be able to deal with the difficulties you meet much more easily than before.

You can keep your petals by pressing the envelope between two pages in a book. When you have experienced a special moment of happiness or success, take out a single petal to mark the occasion. When you have used up all the petals you know that your flower has done its work and it is time to perform the ceremony again, with a different flower.

Another effective way of preserving your healing flower vibrations is by creating a flower essence. This is a simple method that transfers energy patterns into water which can be kept for a long period of time and can be used as a healing remedy. If you have selected your flower from a photograph, purchase a commercial flower remedy from a similar type of flower.

Flowers as meditation aids

You do not need to do a flower reading to benefit from using flowers as mandalas to energise and heal your energy system. You can do the exercise on page 81 using your chosen flower or alternatively by visualisation alone.

Find a comfortable quiet space and lie down on your back, placing your flower on your brow centre in the middle of your forehead. Alternatively you could collect flowers for each chakra centre. You may select these according to the colours, number of petals or shape which you feel mirrors the energy in each chakra.

Creating a healing essence from your flower

Flower essences are often described as 'liquid consciousness' as the life-force vibration is held in a form that can influence and benefit a person's life. Sunlight is essential to the making of flower essences, for it is the action of the sunlight on water that transfers the energy pattern of the flower into the liquid.

Water is the perfect means for capturing the essence of a plant, for water is an excellent carrier of electrical, magnetic, and light energy and is one of the basic elements found in our body.

Scientifically we know that information given to one water molecule will be transmitted in its entirety to all other water molecules with which it comes into contact. So, by transference of energy the vibrational pattern can

Visualisation to energise and balance your chakras

Close your eyes and take some slow deep breaths until you are breathing deeply and rhythmically.

Focus your attention on the base of your spine. Think of this chakra as a beautiful red hibiscus flower. Travel to the centre of the hibiscus and see a channel of light taking you up to the next chakra which is your sacral centre in your pelvic area. Imagine this energy centre as a beautiful deep orange. Feel the orange energy warming you all over. Exhale your past hurts and grief and feel old associations leave you. Move to the centre of this flower and see a channel of light taking you up to your solar-plexus.

Here you find a golden-yellow sunflower. Sense a lightness and brightness in your being and feel the yellow energy of warm sunlight. Take a deep breath and blow out your worries, tension, fears, doubts and apprehensions. Move to the centre of the sunflower and through the channel of light to your heart centre.

Here is a beautiful deep pink rose cradled in green leaves. Breathe in deeply, breathe in the pink and know that love will flow to and from you. Drink in the green energy too and feel more calm and relaxed. Move into the centre of the rose and through the channel of light to your throat centre. A blue delphinium now takes form. Inhale the blue and feel at peace with yourself and the world.

Travel through the blue delphinium into the channel of light and as you come out the other side you see a beautiful iris flower in front of you. As you look at the iris you feel as if all your pains and worries will float away into the sky. The centre of the iris flower draws you inwards and upwards.

You are now at your crown centre, and drink in the energy which comes from a pure white lotus flower. You are filled with perfect love and white light. Keep breathing in the white until you are radiating love and light.

It is time to move your energy back into your physical body, and to do this you need to close the petals of each of the flowers. Start by imagining you are closing the petals of the white lotus, then the deep blue iris. Then move to the blue delphinium, and next close the petals of the rose. Imagine the petals of the sunflower closing and then those of the gerbera. Finally, focus on the red hibiscus but leave one petal open, so that you remain connected to the life-force energy.

When you are ready, open your eyes.

be passed on from molecule to molecule when more water is added. What is so extraordinary is that a single droplet will contain the complete energetic programme.

Seventy-five per cent of the earth's surface is covered by water which in its turn is influenced by celestial bodies. The moon exerts a powerful influence upon the tides and cycles of growth within the plant and animal kingdoms. It also affects the water within our own body, and many of our metabolic rhythms. The vibrations in water are not only a perfect medium for capturing the essence of a flower, they are also able to directly affect our moods and emotions.

Flower essences, unlike essential oils, do not contain any plant material as it is the vibrational patterning that is transferred and diffused through the water molecules. No molecules of the original healing substance or 'mother' tincture are present in the final healing product. This is why normal scientific methods are inappropriate for testing flower essences and it is only by collecting data on the effects of the essences from case studies that we can prove the effectiveness of vibrational healing methods.

As you will only be making a flower essence for your own use, you do not need to worry about making a homoeopathic dilution. These methods are only necessary when making large quantities of flower essences for commercial use.

To capture your flower's healing vibrations in water you will need the following equipment:

* a small clear glass bowl (soup-bowl size)

* a large brown, blue or green glass bottle for your 'mother' tincture

* some brown or blue glass dropper bottles

* pure water – spring, well or from a sacred source

* alcohol – good quality brandy preferably distilled in wooden vats

* labels.

Anyone can make a flower essence, but you need to take a great deal of care and love when doing so or you may not be bottling the right type of vibrations! Try not to touch the flowers and petals as the vibrational pollution from your hands can be transferred to the essence. It is best to try to carry the flowers to the bowl using two pieces of twig or leaves or some other natural object.

If it is possible, make your essence in close proximity to the plant from which it was picked. Choose the early morning or late afternoon to make your flower essence but don't worry if you make it at another time as long as there is bright natural light. Into your clear glass bowl pour pure water until it is approximately two-thirds full. Place your flower gently on the surface of the water and then place the bowl in a protected place in the sunshine. This is necessary as you don't want dirt and other material to be blown into the water.

Spend a few minutes connecting to the plant and ask for its healing vibrations to be transferred into the water. Leave the bowl in direct sunlight for a hour or two. The exact length of time will depend on the strength of the sunshine, but you will have to use your intuition in determining when the essence is ready.

When I make flower essences I like to sit quietly and meditate by the flower while the essence is being solarised. During this time you will become closely connected with the Deva of the flower and given many insights to its purpose and healing energy.

Last year I waited patiently by the flower essence that I was making from a self-seeded buddleia bush in the hope of a butterfly visiting the flowers in my bowl. I really wanted to take a photograph of the visitor for an article I was writing. After an hour not a single insect had visited the essence even though there were hundreds of bees, hoverflies and butterflies flying around the bush. Several times I came back in the hope that they would be seeking other blooms to pollinate, but with no luck. Eventually I decided to remove the essence as it was ready to be bottled. As I put the camera down, a beautiful peacock butterfly alighted on the flowers in the bowl and worked precisely up and down each of the three flower heads. I had learned the lesson that you cannot programme everything to suit your own time-scale. Trust and faith will bring its rewards, but in its own time!

When your essence is ready, using two twigs, lift the flower out of the water. The remaining water is now called a flower infusion from which you will make the 'mother' tincture. If it is not too withered, you may still wish to keep the flower in a vase or bowl. Alternatively, if your flower has thin petals, you can press it between two sheets of absorbent paper in a book. Keep your dried flower in a locket or encapsulate it in plastic and use it in your diary. In this way you will keep it near you.

Making the Mother tincture

You now need to make the mother tincture that will preserve the essence and from which you could make some stock bottles. In order to preserve your essence you need to purchase some good quality alcohol. Brandy is the most commonly used as it is a natural product. It is a good idea to select your brandy carefully, perhaps that which is made in oak casks from the country in which you are making the flower essence.

Fill a large glass bottle half-full with a good alcohol brandy, and add the flower infusion in equal proportions (50 per cent brandy and 50 per cent flower infusion). Label this 'mother tincture of…' and the date and place where it was made.

On the label make a note of the colours of the flower, too. You may have made a flower essence from a flower that has had the vibrational energy of an insect, bird or butterfly. The flower essence made from these will be termed ' bee enhanced' or 'butterfly 'enhanced' 'essence of…'.

Do not keep your flower essences near any electrical or power circuits as they are vibrational essences that will be disturbed by any strong changes in the magnetic field nearby. Also ensure that all bottles are stored away from the light, heat, perfumes, chemicals and aromatics to prevent them from becoming contaminated with other vibrations.

Taking flower essences

There are several ways of taking your flower essence that will enable you to experience the immediate healing affects and to promote long-term healing. You need to tune in to your moods and feelings before using the essence and then concentrate on your thoughts and emotions afterwards. In this way you will become aware of the powerful yet subtle shift of energy within you.

The most usual way to take a flower essence is orally. Drop the essence directly into your mouth, taking care not to touch the dropper with your tongue. A few drops of essence should be taken in the early morning and evening as this is the time you are mentally most relaxed and sensitive to the vibrations in the essence. Many times, essences work through the unconscious in our dreams. Recording any vivid or important dreams will reveal how the essences are changing your consciousness.

Flower essences can also be added to natural drinks as diluting them will not alter their strength.

You can use your flower essence on the foot reflexes and accupressure points on the body or you can hold the bottle containing the flower essence directly on a chakra centre and allow healing to take place.

You can also add flower essences to bath water, and I would recommend you burn an appropriate coloured candle while relaxing in the bath to reinforce the effect. You can use flower essences both in the bath and as a spray mist. In a warm (not too hot) a bath, place a few drops of flower essence. Remember that the vibrational pattern is transferred from one water molecule to another, so that every molecule of water in the bath will be imprinted with the information. So it is the quality of what you put into the water and not the quantity that is important. To make a spray mist, get a bottle with a spray or pump and fill it with pure still water. Mix in a few drops of flower essence. You can use the spray as a body mist or room spray. By inhaling the purified air you will take in the healing energy through your lungs and skin.

After making your flower essence you should take a few drops straight away, but you can also use it on other special occasions especially if you have been guided to do so by the Deva of the flower.

I made a flower essence with a group of people and while the flowers were infused in sunlight we joined hands around the plant. During this meditation we learned that the flowers contain spiritually uplifting and transformative qualities. It also came to light that we should all take the flower essence simultaneously during the full solar eclipse at eleven minutes past eleven o'clock on the eleventh day of August 1999.

Selecting a commercially made essence

Steve Johnson, of the Alaskan flower-essence project describes the development of flower essences like this: 'Flower-essence research is a living, ongoing process that is ultimately linked to the collective unconscious of humankind. The healing potential that nature holds is enormous. As we increase contact with nature through the use of flower essences and other natural systems of healing, our understanding for this potential will grow.'

Making a flower essence from a living flower embodies the complete healing system you need, but if you do not have a real flower you could work with a commercially made range. Unfortunately flower essences, like other remedies, can only treat specific symptoms, all be they emotional and mental rather than physical ones. It is therefore important that you take time in identifying the right ones.

There has been a recent explosion in the number of flower essences available from every part of the world. Today anyone wishing to buy a flower essence has a daunting task finding the right one to take. Many people will go to a vibrational healer or flower-essence practitioner who has studied flower essences in depth. Since there are so many ranges using thousands of flowers, you need to identify which group of flowers would be the most suitable for your needs.

If, however, you have done a flower reading you will know exactly which flower energy you require. Your first priority should be to find an essence made from the same flower, although this may not be the same variety. If you cannot find your flower listed in a flower essence directory, you need to find two essences, one that reflects the negative state and one that reflects the positive qualities of your choice.

A flower of a similar shape and family is likely to reflect the same area of disharmony in your system, while one of the same colour would contain the healing vibrations you need. For the second flower essence it is a good idea to look under the index for positive qualities you need to attract into your life. If several flowers are listed, select the one that grows in the same part of the world where you live in preference to the others.

Your flower reading may have touched on several problem areas needing to be brought into alignment. A good way of deciding which flower essences to use is to start by looking for those essences originating in the same part of the world as where you live. It is well known that plants and food grown locally provide the right physical nourishment and vibrational energy for the people living in that area. (This is the prime benefit of eating organically grown local produce.) The plants are stronger and better adapted to the soil and climate and thus more potent in their nutrients.

If the qualities you are seeking are not represented in the local flower-essence range you will have to look further afield. Flower essences from each part of the world and specific climatic conditions have identifiable themes. Knowledge of these can be of great assistance when seeking out those flowers with sympathetic healing patterns.

Flower essence auras

The quality of light we receive into our body has a direct relationship to the part of the world where we live. The proportions of spectral colours in the sunlight have a profound effect on our primary functions, energy levels and health. In hot, dry regions sunlight is more direct and intense so that the light literally glows white, while in cooler climates the rays of light are biased towards a cooler blue. The intensity and quality of the light vibrations are also constantly changing with the seasons and provide us with signals for our internal body clock, inner rhythms and metabolic cycles. This regulation of our internal energy system harmonises our body systems with that of the natural world.

It is generally agreed that who we are is a result of both genetics and environmental factors. The quality of light vibrations we received into our system at birth will have had a profound effect on our physical and mental faculties. We call this our 'vibrational genetic make-up'. The light vibrations and colours entering our system at any particular time will have an on-going relationship with our health and can alter the course of our life. We can use flowers to reveal our inherited pre-dispositions but also use their healing power to help us find the balance between these inherited traits and current environmental factors.

The colours of flowers in each climatic environment mirror the quality of the light vibrations entering our system. Every ecosystem has flowers that reflect all the rainbow colours, but the intensity of the hues will differ greatly. In warm, dry conditions flowers are more likely to be coloured hot red, orange, gold and violet whereas those found in temperate damp zones, will have petals of clear light colours. Most of the flowers in higher latitudes will have softer and cooler colours in the pink, light-green, blue and lilac range. The nearer the poles you travel, the more the petals will reflect pure white light.

As plants have a group (rather than an individual) consciousness, the flowers growing in one particular environment reflect a combined radiant floral aura. The auras of flower-essence ranges are most revealing. Each range is made up of a variety of notes, which together create a musical melody linking in to the earth's own planetary song. The floral auras surround the earth with a pulsating force-field of light energy which acts as a harmonic protection and contributes to global harmony.

Choosing a range of flower essences

The most difficult question facing an individual or practitioner who wishes to purchase and use flower essences, is to know which ones to use. Do you work with one particular range only, or select remedies from several different ranges? Most people choose a range with which they feel a certain affinity but this presumes you are familiar with all the possibilities. At other times one ends up choosing an essence from a well-known range and ignoring others that may be more appropriate to our needs. If we understand the healing themes of different ranges of essences, we are much better equipped to make an informed choice.

In order to lead a full and healthy life, we need to find a vibrational balance that is relevant both to our inherited and present energetic make-up. These factors are important when choosing an individual or range of flower essences, as you need to find those that contain sympathetic patterns to your inner vibrations.

At birth, the electro-magnetic vibrations transmitted through our parents have a remarkable effect on our physical body. People born in the poles have larger heads in proportion to their bodies while those born in the tropics have smaller heads in relation to their body size. In temperate zones the proportion of the head is neither small nor large compared with body size.

Climate also has a direct relationship with the development of other parts of our psyche and our life-style. In colder regions where we spend more time indoors, we tend to follow more intellectual pursuits and the cold climate is mirrored in our inward-looking life-style. Less emphasis is placed on externalised emotional expression and physical activities. This is why people who live in cold climates are generally thought of as being more cool, calm and undemonstrative. In contrast, cultures that develop in warm climates are much more outward oriented, both physically and emotionally. Their mental pursuits are often interpreted in a practical way. Spiritual life is abundant in all parts of the world, but the forms or rites and rituals will also follow this theme: in warm areas religious festivals and rituals are more lavish and colourful, whereas northern rites tend to be more refined and internalised.

If the quality of light in the area of our birth can have such a profound affect on our physical body, it must also have a similar effect on the growth and development of plants. There will be a direct relationship between our energetic make-up and that of the plants growing in the same location. The philosophy of 'Gaia' can help us understand this relationship better.

The word 'Gaia' was ancient Greek for 'mother earth', and rose out of the view that the earth is a living organism and that plants mirror the living earth. In the plant world the type, shape and colour of plants become dominant depending on the area of the earth in which they grow. In polar regions the earth is cold and the ground contracted, so light is more important, whereas in the tropics the soil is warm and living so the earth energies predominate. Plants become contracted and grow close to the ground in the polar areas, while becoming expanded and open in the tropics. In cold climates the flower reaches up into the light away from the leaves and roots, while in warmer places the flower is encircled by the leaves and becomes an integral part of the plant.

We can conclude that the magnetism in the earth and the quality of the rays of sunlight shape the internal and external form of all living things. What is more, we can make a direct correlation between the energy patterns of plants found growing in the same geographical area of our birth and our body. We will also have a sympathetic harmony with plants that grow in the area where we live, for they will provide us with the best type of food and medicine.

Essences for travellers

The close links between our own form and that of flowers growing in the same environment suggests that we should be only using remedies made from flowers grown locally. However this can cause a problem in our highly mobile society.

For those of you who have moved away from the country of your birth or to a different geographical location you will have to find the right balance between your inherent energy needs at birth, and your present requirements.

If you feel a strong connection with the area of your birth, it would be a good idea to work with flowers local to that area. These vibrations will help you develop and fortify your strengths and talents and help you realise your full potential. If, on the other hand, you have been living in another place for a long time, flowers growing in that area will help you adapt to your new environment more easily.

Many people today are constantly travelling and in this case it would be wise to use flower essences that link to the particular part of your being that needs attention. So, you could choose a flower from the hot countries to improve your sexual relationships, while using one from more temperate zones to balance negative mental traits. Tropical rainforests provide remedies especially good for emotional and communication problems. Flowers growing in the polar regions or high in the mountains reflect white light into your system and are thus spiritually uplifting. These flowers are especially useful for world travellers as they bring your body rhythms back into alignment and balance all areas of the psyche.

Healing themes of different flower essences of the world

While we find an array of shapes and colours in flowers in every part of the world, the intensity of the colours and the forms of the flowers reflect special healing themes. Flowers from particular areas are therefore more appropriate to healing certain parts of our psyche but also radiate energy patterns required to maintain ecological harmony in that area of the world.

Polar flowers

Light is of particular importance at the poles, for it is the driving force for growth in these areas. Sun, moon and stars, as well as light from other cosmic forces, are extremely potent and pure. The sun shines continuously for six months of the year, while the other six are destined to dark. Stars neither rise nor set at the poles but are fixed for the whole year with the Pole star at the zenith. It is therefore not surprising that plants in the poles also yield star-like flowers.

Flowering plants explode into a myriad of colours during the short growing season, but the quality of the colours is translucent and delicate. Flowers from this environment connect to the crown chakra, giving us inspiration and upliftment of the spirit through transformation from above.

Tropical flowers

Heat produces growth and expansion. The strength of this vibrant, warm earth energy creates gigantic forms so that the flowers in the tropics are open, expansive and hot coloured. The pigments are deep and rich while being opaque and bright. What would be a herbaceous plant in a temperate climate becomes a giant in the tropics, often turning into shrubs and trees.

Flowers take on weird forms often mimicking organs of our body. The flowers from these hot climates contain an upward-moving energy excellent for healing the body and closely connected emotional states.

This soaring upward force in the tropics has literally lifted some flowers off the ground into the air. They make their homes in holes in tree trunks or on branches in the leaf canopy. These flowers are mainly orchids and some ferns are also nourished by the moisture in the air. Flowers that have been liberated in this way have made a major step in evolution and it is these essences that we can use to open our heart chakra so we can express to our finer emotions of unconditional love and empathy. Air is the element of the mind and orchid essences can link our open heart chakra to our intuition and higher mind.

Flowers from hot dry regions

The earth in hot sunny climates releases a great deal of energy and heat. It pushes upwards from the ground, filling flowers with a tremendous magnetic force. These flowers are hot, vibrant colours such as red, orange, gold and violet which indicate the strength of their vibrations and radiant energy of the sun. In desert conditions, the outer forms of plants become thick and hard to the touch in order to prevent dehydration. The trapped energy held in these plants becomes highly concentrated in the few flowers that appear. These flowers are immensely powerful in releasing trapped energy from your body. The colour of the transforming power is revealed by their colouring, so red flowers will move blocked sexual energy, yellow can transform mental energy, and white or violet indicate spiritual movement.

Dryness is linked to the element of air, which has a strong relationship with our spiritual body. So, flowers growing in hot dry conditions contain physically strengthening power but also provide you with strength and determination to follow your spiritual path.

Temperate zones

The forces of light and earth are more equally balanced in the temperate parts of the earth. Flowers are neither totally enveloped by the plant nor differentiated by rising far above their leaves. The hues of these flowers are clear and bright, without the heaviness of the tropical colours. The spectrum of colour energy in these areas works through the mind – the force that binds our spirit and body together in this life on earth.

It is also possible to select a flower essence from a commercial range according to the geographical area where they are made. The location from where the flowers are selected will have a particular resonance with different parts of our being according to the elements to which they relate.

Flowers linked to the five natural elements

The five natural elements are the basic building-blocks of life from which everything is formed. The elements reveal themselves in the basic geometric patterns of atoms and molecules which create the external form and structure of matter. These shapes have different qualities and can be linked to the five elements of earth, air, fire, water and ether. Different combinations of these elements are found in living things, but it is thought that only in humankind are all five elements found.

Each element links to a different part of our being. The physical body has a closeness to the earth as this is the element of the greatest density, whereas our emotions are in tune with the mercurial nature of water. Our mind is connected to the air element while our spirit corresponds closely to the element of ether which has the finest vibrations of all.

In the plant world, the five elements are separated so that different plants have an affinity with one particular element depending on the location in which it grows. Within each local environment you will find flowers related to each of the five elements.

Flowers found growing on mountain tops and at the North and South Poles are able to balance our spirit as they are linked to the element of ether. On the slopes and temperate zones of the world are found flowers that harmonise the mind and reflect the air element. In the tropics and lowlands grow flowers that have an affinity with our emotions and physical body. Deserts relate to the body through the element of fire, while our emotions relate to the element of water. This makes flowers that grow in or near water particularly beneficial to balancing our moods and helpful in times of emotional crisis. Flowers growing in woodlands and forests link with the higher mind and finer emotions through the element of earth. Their healing works through the heart centre, encouraging the qualities of compassion, empathy and understanding.

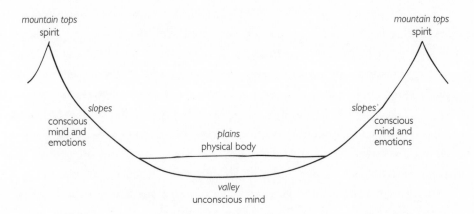

The place where you find your flower, either for a flower reading or to make a flower essence, will give you a strong indication as to which part of your psyche it will most influence. Flowers found growing on the forest floor, in valleys or on plains will have a dramatic effect on the physical body. Those found in the countryside where there are rolling hills will have more resonance with your emotional body, while those found higher up the slopes will have a strong effect on the mind. If you find your flower at the top of a mountain it will send its healing vibrations into your spiritual body.

If you wish to create your own range of flower essences or wish to use a selection from a flower essence manufacturer, the geographical area where the flowers are found will guide you to the overall benefits of the remedies.

Four case studies of flower reading

In the following brief case studies you will be able to follow the steps involved in giving a flower reading and see how the messages conveyed by the flower is relevant to the person who chose them. You will also get an idea of the different ways you can use a flower to bring its healing vibrations into your life.

1. Julie   *Flower chosen: pink hydrangea*

Julie is a single mother. She has a lovely daughter of four years who she has been caring for since her partner left two years ago. Julie feels she has gone through great emotional and financial hardship but recently she is feeling more optimistic about the future. She is looking for a place in a nursery for the child and has applied for a training grant through a local enterprise scheme.

Julie picked a pink hydrangea. This was a large, soft floppy flower-head that formed a round ball of small flowers. The bush where it was picked was full of flowers and growing in the full sun amongst numerous other flowers in the garden. Each flower had a blush of colour which varied from deep pink, through to very pale pink and lilac. After a short while the flowers started to wither and their paper thin petals wilted so that the flower head lost its shape when left on the table. There were many butterflies in the area but none were seen to pollinate this flower.

READING

General flower shape – round orb

This shape reveals a person with many different facets that have to be unified in order for them to reveal their full potential. Julie has many talents that need to be brought together to create a beautiful whole. The flower-head is made up from many flowers so this person needs the understanding and love of sympathetic people in order to feel secure. Julie needs to find support from people who understand her position – her family, friends or other single mothers.

Location and growing conditions – sunny position on a prolific bush in a garden

The fertile location shows a place where there is opportunity to grow and flourish. There are, however, lots of other plants and flowers competing for the same resources. The hydrangea flower reflects a person who feels that they are one of many with no particular distinguishing talents so they may feel that they do not stand out in the crowd. This might manifest in a feeling of frustration and low self-esteem. The flower certainly suggests that Julie's desire to undertake a course of study is the right way forward for it could solve her financial problems as well as build her self-confidence.

Texture – paper thin and easily wilting

The softness and thin quality of the petals of the hydrangea flower show an extremely soft and sensitive soul who hasn't much resilience especially when separated from the people she loves. Perhaps this person has been used by others and left without sustenance. This was the case when Julie's partner left her to cope on her own.

Colour – pale and translucent colours; each small flower-head had different colours

The pale quality of the colours shows that healing should take place at a deep level, in the more subtle areas of being. The colours pink and lilac also reinforce the idea that the flower reflects a person who has a great deal of love to give, but who needs to be appreciated for herself. When this happens the spirit will be healed. Julie should surround herself with pastel colours in her dress and home to promote this spiritual healing. Making a flower essence from the hydrangea would also help these healing light vibrations to work.

Aroma – no apparent aroma

Pale flowers often have a very faint aroma or one which is too fine for our sense organs to perceive. In this case it is the colour vibrations that hold the key to healing and these colours should be introduced into Julie's life in order to facilitate healing.

Insect energy – no direct connection seen

Although there were a number of butterflies around this bush, none were seen to alight on this particular flower. This would indicate that there are changes in the air but not just yet. The shape of the individual flowers also suggests tiny pink wings, and in this case may connect to the angelic kingdom rather than the insect world. Julie should call upon her guardian angel to assist her. Transformation will come with her inner faith and knowing that everything will be all right.

As the flower which Julie picked withered quite quickly, she decided to make a flower essence right way to hold its healing vibrations. I also placed a piece of pink quartz crystal into the water as this stone would enhance the protective qualities of the essence. Julie took the essence daily for a month and after this time reported that during this time she had intuitively handed over her problems to a higher force, rather than trying to sort out everything herself. This had brought her a great sense of relief, and she had every faith that she would receive the help and support she needed. Not long afterwards, a place in a nursery became available which allowed Julie to pursue her application for a study grant. This also materialised and Julie now attends college part-time. Julie also bought a scarf with the same colouring as her hydrangea – pinks and lilacs and she wears this when she is feeling fragile or depressed. In all Julie says she feels she is coming out of the grieving process and can look towards a loving and bright future.

2. Donald   *Flower chosen: A bulrush and pampas flower*

Donald is an exceptionally bright young man who is studying computer science at university. Unfortunately he was suffering greatly from stress and was unable to sleep or relax. He lives with his mother, and their relationship was getting frayed. Donald needed some guidance on how to reduce his stress and resolve his relationship with this mum.

It was winter when Donald did his flower reading. His first choice was a single bulrush flower and then he found a pampas-grass flower. The bulrush was a single upright flower which had gone to seed. It consisted of an upright spike that was cylindrical in shape and dark brown. The rush resembled a bottle brush, but the texture was soft and furry – much like the coat of an animal like a mole. The pampas flower was also upright but picked from a bush that had many flowers. Unlike the bulrush, it was soft and feathery and pale in colour.

The bulrush as his first choice will reveal his present situation and feelings, while the pampas flower will indicate the potential for change.

READING

General flower shapes – pointed and upright

Flowers that point upwards to the sky generally reveal aspiration qualities and the desire to improve yourself mentally and spiritually. Both these flowers show a strong will and person who is focused on one particular thing. This is certainly the case with Donald who has been concentrating on his studies to the exclusion of other things. Often the person reflected by a pointed flower does not readily show their emotions, and flowers that are air pollinated reveal someone particularly biased towards solving their problems with their mind.

Location and growing conditions

The bulrush was growing in water and, although surrounded by other bulrushes, this was the only flower left. The pampas flower was growing in a rockery on a bush with lots of similar flowers. The bulrush had its roots in water showing a strong emotional connection, but it also strives upwards towards the air element which is the mind and spirit. This shows a person who has deep feelings that they may be bottling up.

The pampas grass, on the other hand, grows in dry soil in rocky places, showing that the person probably received little support during childhood – and yet these people do not lose their humanity and manage to retain their softness and openness. As the pampas grass was the second choice, the message this flower brought was that Donald could still obtain his goals and high ideals through gentleness and sharing with others. Even if he had little parental support when young, he can still flourish and flower without harbouring resentment.

Texture – bulrush was soft and furry but rigid; pampas was upright but soft and feathery

The bulrush appeared hard and unyielding and yet it had a protective soft covering like fur. This reflects a person who feels like they are in a strait-jacket and have to appear to be upright and in control, when in fact they need to feel secure and protected. The softness and lightness of the pampas flower promote a lightness of spirit so that they don't take life so seriously. This is the healing potential offered by the flower reading.

Colour – bulrush was dark brown; pampas was pale brown to creamy white

Brown is the colour of the earth. It is nurturing and safe but also can be restrictive and its comforting vibrations can prevent one leaving the nest. Donald still lives with his mother in the family home. So, although this may be convenient it may also be holding back his development as a mature adult. The pampas flower indicates a change from the brown to the lighter colour. The creamy white indicates a liberating and freeing action that will bring relief from tension and stress.

Aroma – no apparent aroma on either

These flowers are both wind pollinated, and so Donald should open his mind to new and different ways of doing things.

Insect energy – damselfly on bulrush

A beautifully coloured damselfly was seen alighting on the bulrush and is a messenger of metamorphosis and transformation. Donald has yet to find his wings and fly. When this happens, he will be able to do his own dance but still visit his mother and allow love to flow between them.

Donald was very surprised by the accuracy of the reading, and even while we were discussing his situation he was unconsciously stroking the velvety bulrush. When I drew his attention to this fact, he said that he had always loved animals and that being in their presence had a relaxing and calming affect on him. He told me that their family dog had died several years previously, and he would now discuss the possibility of getting another, with his mother. He also bought a picture of a beautiful damselfly hovering over water, which he hung on the wall. Whenever he felt tired from study, Donald would use this picture for its calming but inspirational qualities.

The pampas flower signified freedom to Donald, but he knew he had to stay at home until he could support himself financially. At the end of the summer term he decided to go on a working holiday on a cattle ranch in America. On his return he was delighted to find that his mother had arranged a visit to the local dogs' home, where they fell in love with an abandoned young terrier. Donald reports a big release of tension at home and, although still working hard, is taking a much more relaxed attitude to his work. He says that he can always become a dog-walker if he doesn't pass his exams!

3. Linda   *Flower chosen: tiger lily*

Linda is a married women in her sixties. Her youngest daughter has recently left home and moved to another town, so that the house feels particularly empty now that all three children have left home. Linda is quite an emotional person with the tendency to lose her temper. She is worried that her irritability will be directed towards her husband, especially now that they are on their own. She would like to return to her music as she was once quite a good piano player. Linda thinks the music would help calm and soothe her soul.

Linda has chosen a tiger lily for her flower. This is a beautiful open flower with stamens full of thick orange pollen. The flower is a golden orange with deep red speckles. This particular flower was growing in a sheltered part of the garden at an angle with its head turned towards the ground so that the petals rolled back to allow the stamens to hang free. She thought it resembled a jester's hat.

General flower shape – downturned trumpet

The lily family has a life theme of feminine expression. The trumpet shape shows an outward flow of energy indicating that the person is mature and should use the talents that they have already developed. The fact that the shape suggested a jester's hat is particularly interesting as this would suggest a person who has been hiding their true feelings behind frivolity and laughter.

Location and growing conditions

The lily was growing in a protected area of the garden in a clump. This location reflects someone who has led a sheltered life and has been surrounded by a close-knit family or community. The flower Linda picked was leaning out from the bunch, showing a need to break free of the mould in order to establish individuality and affording her the potential to attract new energy into her life.

Texture – waxy petals

The texture of this flower was not as striking as the colour, but, nevertheless, the soft waxy nature of the petals suggests a softness and fullness linked to the feminine principle. The spongy texture could also indicate water trapped within the body, which is often the case with older women.

Colour – deep golden orange with dark red speckles

The dramatic markings of the tiger lily are very reminiscent of a tiger – hence its name. This suggests someone who is predatory and aggressive but also reveals a person who is strong and clever. Red energy has always been linked to anger and the speckles would indicate someone who is experiencing bouts of anger. The red spots suggest an irritating rash.

Aroma – powerful and haunting aroma

The strong aroma of the tiger lily is hidden deep within the flower so that you really have to stick your nose into it in order to smell its perfume, but after leaving the lily in a vase for some time the aroma began to pervade the air. This type of aroma suggests that the person only reveals their true potential to those who take time to appreciate them.

Insect energy – no direct connection seen

The flower was not visited by an insect during the time Linda was looking at it, but the fact that the stamens were heavily laden with pollen and extended outwards from the flower, indicates that communication is an important issue for Linda and the key to balancing the aggressive tendencies with feminine strength. A return to piano playing would be an important step which would help her relax and promote her enjoyment of life.

Linda put her flower into a vase and placed it on her dressing table, where it stayed for several days. She felt that the flower had an immediately uplifting effect which made her smile. The rich aroma was calming but also made her feel more feminine and sexy. As Linda wanted to keep her flower in the vase, I suggested she take tiger lily essence made by the Flower Essence Society in California. She took the essence by mouth for a fortnight and then continued to add a few drops to her bath every few days during the following weeks. The lily flower essence had an immediate calming effect, and over a period of time Linda came to realise that now her family had left home she and her husband could now renew their bond and love for each other. She also came to understand that her purpose in life was not only connected with serving other people, but that she was a valuable member of the family too. She could now nurture and care for herself without feeling guilty.

4. Wendy   *Flower chosen: honeysuckle*

Wendy is a woman in her late forties who lives on her own. Her high-powered job in the city requires a great deal of travel at home and abroad. Wendy has never been married although she has had some long-term relationships. She feels she never seems to find a 'Mr Right', someone who can accept both her independence and the demands of her job. Wendy finds her job tiring but is very sociable and seldom stays at home.

Wendy was attracted to a creamy yellow honeysuckle flower from a bush that was clambering over several other plants. She said that it was the fragrance of the flower that attracted her attention although there were other more showy flowers nearby.

READING

General flower shape – cluster of tiny flowers

The honeysuckle flower is made up of several tiny flowers each with a single petal that has divided into two, allowing the stamens to reveal themselves. This shape can be related to the number one which carries the power of unity. The cluster of tiny flowers work together as one, bringing in separate energies to work for the good of the whole. The central theme, therefore, indicates the need to bring diverse areas of this person back to the centre.

Location and growing condition – climbing

This plant is a prolific creeper and will use any other plant or object in its path as a means of support. Honeysuckle does not damage other plants although the weight of its enthusiasm could become difficult to bear. The growth of this flower suggests someone who clings to the past and the good times, closing themselves to the possibilities of new relationships. It gives Wendy the message that she should be more receptive and open to the present and not get stuck by feelings of regret.

Texture – this flower is very fragile and has delicate petals and stamens

Although the texture reflects someone who is very sweet natured and sensitive, it also suggests a person who is extremely resilient as they can thrive well in any conditions. Perhaps Wendy needs to show her softer side and vulnerability without fear of losing her energy and dynamism.

Colour – the flower was a cream and pink-orange colour

These colours encourage warmth and responsiveness in female sexuality and an integration of soul warmth and bodily passion. They will also help Wendy relax and enjoy a relationship without the expectation of long-term commitment. In this way she won't be sending out signals of desperation.

Aroma – honey-sweet fragrance

The aroma of this flower holds the key to its healing vibration for it strengthens the brow and crown chakras. This means that it helps problems related to memory and balances the hemispheres of the brain. Wendy was particularly tired from a hard week at work when she chose this flower. In the longer term, the honeysuckle contains energy that stimulates flexibility in the mind, body and spirit and awakens psychic abilities.

Insect energy – possible pollination by moths

Although Wendy did not see any insect pollinate this flower, the honeysuckle flower changes its shape and colour daily in order to attract butterflies and night-flying moths to assist in pollination. This ability brings an energy pattern that helps you adapt more easily to your environment and situation. The possibility of the flower being visited by moths (night-flying insects), suggests healing energy in the feminine aspect, also helping her to acknowledge her shadow self. By accepting and integrating both masculine and feminine aspects within us we become whole and connected.

Wendy loved the shape and scent of the honeysuckle and decided to float the flower in a bowl of water on her coffee table. To this she added a few drops of Honeysuckle Remedy from the Bach Flower essence range. She took time over the next few days to sit and meditate for ten minutes before and after work. By calming her active mind, she tuned in to her inner self and discovered that she needed to change her attitude to relationships and expectations from a partner. Wendy also used the honeysuckle essence in her bath, and allowed herself to relax and spend time in her own company, at home. Wendy decided to redecorate her living room in a rich creamy yellow as she felt this colour helped her to become less aggressive and more relaxed in her social interactions. She reported that her friends had noticed a change in her, and that she was less aggressive and more sensitive to approaches by men. Within a year, Wendy found someone with whom she felt comfortable and she says that she would never have been able to develop such an intimate and loving relationship without the help of the lovely flower. They have now planted a honeysuckle bush in a planter outside their bedroom window.

From these four cases studies you will have discovered how a flower reading can work in a very personal and remarkable way. In Donald's case, the insect energy carried by the bulrush was the most significant factor which brought into his consciousness his love of animals. By developing this natural connection he was able to ease his stress and to become more independent. On the other hand it was the colour and markings of the Tiger Lily that pinpointed Linda's state of mind and helped her understand her changed emotional and social situation.

Often, during my flower reading workshops two people have chosen the same type of flower and it is quite extraordinary how two similar flowers can carry different messages and healing power for each individual. In a world where we are so keen to put people and their problems into neat categories it is rewarding to find a simple natural method by which we can empower and facilitate our own inner healing.

PART 4

Healing the planet

Network of light energy

The ladder of ascent

Flower colours in relation to your life's work

Flowers as an aid to evolution

Our crystalline planet

Healing for the new era

The spiritual renaissance

Flower reading chart

Healing the planet

Our personal relationship with flowers can renew our connection and respect for the natural world but plants also play an even more important role. Flowering plants not only provide sustenance for living things but also nourish the earth itself.

We can regard plants as the outer expression of the earth so that the soul of the earth is revealed by the plants themselves. Plants do not have their own internal rhythms like we do, instead they pulsate with the rhythms of the universal mind and cosmic forces. These harmonious forces are revealed in the perfectly formed geometrical patterns and shapes of flowers. It is in the flower that light energy from above and magnetic energy from below ground is united, creating a flow of life-nurturing vibrations in and around the earth.

The earth can be viewed as having a body like our own with different parts of it corresponding to different parts of our being. The poles can be regarded as the head and higher mind, while the equator has the same function as our solar plexus. The temperate zones are similar to our temperament which expresses our emotions and feelings. The equator correlates to our solar-plexus centre which is the seat of our personal power. It links strongly to our ego and central nervous system.

The lower part of our body, including our digestive and sexual organs are represented by the southern hemisphere. This also includes our lower limbs and base chakra which affects our physical strength and mobility. The northern hemisphere is linked to the upper body, heart, chest and upper limbs. It is the area that represents our mental faculties. Both southern and northern climates reflect the energy in our heart although the southern areas are more closely linked to our feelings and desires. Our finer emotions that work through the higher mind are reflected in northern latitudes.

The correspondence between our own energetic make-up and that of the earth is not a new idea. The German esoteric biologist, Gerbert Grohmann, as far back as 1929 wrote a wonderful book that helps us understand the link

The growth patterns and colouring of flowers growing in different latitudes have a sympathetic resonance with different parts of our being. The auric colours of different flower essence ranges shows a bias towards certain colour wave lengths

between the earth and our own bodies – *Die Pflanze* (*The Plant*). In this book Grohmann describes the delicate arctic flowers as sparkling like crystals. He says that the arctic flowers are visible thought pictures of the earth in the regions which represent the head.

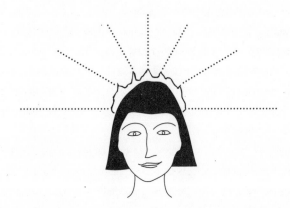

In this drawing the polar cap is linked to the top of the head. It is seen as a carpet of crystals that reflects rainbows of light around the world and into all parts of our being

He goes on to describe how the flowering impulse in the tropics is similar to the metabolic system in humankind. Flowers take on forms that look much like organs, with heavy, earthy, sensual colours and scents. The temperate zones correspond to the rhythmic system in man, such as the circulation, digestive and respiratory processes.

When the earth is in harmony, plants are strong and healthy and there is a balanced eco-system. Areas where there is tension and movement of energy underground will reveal themselves by diseases and deformed plant growth.

The plant kingdom is not, however, entirely dependent on the earth because its main energy source is sunlight. This primal energy empowers plants with a cosmic force that ebbs and flows according to the earth's own needs. At a time when the earth is going through major structural and evolutionary upheaval, it is this energetic force, I believe, that will be able to bring all the planetary systems into harmony once more.

Network of light energy

In the formation of this planet from a gaseous mass, light energy from the sun was absorbed and stored deep within its structure. So the earth itself is made up of light energy. We get a glimpse of this hidden light energy in the fiery eruptions of volcanoes and the light-reflecting qualities of gemstones and crystals which grow deep within.

The earth receives energy from the sun – and, in fact, all energy subsequently emitted from the earth is a result of the sun's warming and penetrating rays. This powerful energy is released from the earth in the form of heat and magnetic vibrations. The plant kingdom draws up magnetic energy from the earth and at the same time absorbs light rays from the sun. Through special magical powers, plants transform this energy into a harmonising and balancing force that creates an environment in which all life can thrive.

The whole life of a plant is dedicated to light, and it is in the flower that there is the highest concentration of life-force energy. This life-force is shaped into an electro-magnetic pattern. Like crystals and snowflakes, flowers have inherent symmetry and their forms are created out of the basic geometrical shapes found in all matter. The energy in flowers is not inert, and the light energy absorbed by the flower radiates outwards in a harmonious pattern.

The German astronomer Kepler suggests that the lower earthly realms contain something spiritual which is quickened through geometric harmonic relationship with the celestial rays of light. It encodes in the colour and aroma of the flower the blue-print that is to be transmitted. This is very much like a note in music and, indeed, there is evidence that flowers emit sounds. These notes combine to create a vibrational frequency or melody that forms a connecting network of energy around the earth. In Aboriginal traditions in Australia, the world itself was 'sung' into being and the ancient songlines demarcate different geographical areas on this continent. This network of vibrational energy is a powerful evolutionary force both for us as individuals and as a race.

The ladder of ascent

Evolution does not only apply to the physical world, but also to the spirit. Plants reflect the universal consciousness by allowing the universal forces to flow through them unhindered. As humans we have to work harder to establish this universal connection because we have developed an ego that separates the body from the spirit. The analogy of droplets joining together to form the ocean is often used to describe the natural yearning of our spiritual aspect – the soul – to return to its source.

Everything in this universe is in a state of change and evolution towards something more refined and our soul is also moving towards a state of harmony and perfection. By mirroring our soul, flowers can help us identify our own evolutionary path and help us increase and raise our vibrations.

The energetic impulses of a plant are concentrated in the flowering tip which also carries the potential blue-print for future development. These are revealed in the shape of the flower which follows one of the universal symmetrical patterns. The colour and aroma of the flower contains these transformative codes and can help us move our own energy and break through to another level of consciousness.

If the flower you have selected for your reading was a bud, this will indicate that your soul is still in the early stages of maturity. The bud needs to unfurl in order for you to blossom and make full use of your gifts and talents. Perhaps something or someone has been holding you back. In this case you should look at the environment in which you picked your flower in order to discover what this obstacle might be. Maybe you have been crowded out by others or someone else has been sapping your energy. Your reading will also help you identify ways to nurture yourself and the tools in life that will best guide you towards your true soul's purpose.

A more open flower indicates someone who is just coming into their own. This means that you are on the right path and you should make full use of your talents. The central theme of your flower indicated by its shape can indicate the area of life where you should be concentrating your efforts. The quality of the colour will indicate whether this should be in the physical, emotional or mental realms.

Flower colours in relation to your life's work

Different colours in flowers reflect aspects about our life work as follows:

Pale or transparent your spiritual search and developing your sensitivity to subtle vibrations, mediumship or personal vision

Light clear creative and charitable pursuits

Bright strong emotional strength and mental energy. Use these for pursuing your goals and achieving stable and loving relationships

Rich deep colours physical energy for a new project or to get through difficulties

If your flower is fully open with lots of pollen, you are in full bloom and flowering as an individual. Enjoy who you are and what you have achieved so far. Relax and enjoy this time of celebration and, like the flower, let others come to you for love, knowledge and healing.

A flower that is wilting may indicate a lack of energy, lack of nourishment or even exhaustion. The colour of a wilted flower will indicate in what area of your life you lack support. A dark-coloured flower corresponds to a lack of proper nutrition, while a pale flower shows lack of spiritual nourishment.

Sometimes you may select a flower that is going to seed. The petals may be dropping or have withered and the ovary is swollen. This explosive force indicates a change will come very soon. At this stage the flower is bursting with potential to move on to the next stage. You need to look at your life and discover which areas have served you well and what lessons you have learned. This will enable you to cast off the chains that are preventing you from moving on. An open flower indicates a need to try out new things, learn and experiment so that you widen your outlook on life.

Flowers as an aid to evolution

Most people think of evolution as a slow progressive process whereby living things change bit by bit as a result of environmental demands. In fact, from the study of evolution we discover that things evolve in a dramatic and sometimes surprising way.

In the past we have seen that the major steps in evolution involve a huge jump or shift in emphasis. Instead of progressing up the ladder step by step, often consciousness is lifted to the top of the ladder by a completely different route.

It is natural to suppose that plants were the first inhabitants of the earth, and that the animal kingdom was the natural progression of higher consciousness which evolved from plants. Unfortunately this convenient model is untrue, for there is evidence of animal life on this planet long before plants made their appearance. This could mean that some plants are more evolved than some animal life, for nature is full of surprises. What we do know is that there was a time when plants flourished while other kingdoms lay dormant.

This discovery challenges conventional evolutionary thinking especially where it concerns our own origins. Instead of progressively developing from a species of ape, archaeological finds have unearthed evidence that we may have evolved from a totally different species altogether. Perhaps humankind, or even some humans, evolved through different means.

Rudolph Steiner suggests that evolution is not just a matter of past developments merely being repeated and refined. He suggests that future developments are also hinted at and anticipated before they happen. Each stage of evolution goes through an 'over-ripe' stage; the impulse for development is already implanted in the previous stage. Eventually this energy has to find expression and it breaks through. This is similar to a seed pod that is about to burst. The seeds, or potential, are held within until the moment of release.

If we go along with this idea, we can see that in our own lives this means our personal development and our soul's evolution can take place in a series of transformative leaps. We need challenges in order to make us change and grow for if we stay sitting comfortably in a rut the energy within us stagnates and becomes blocked. If we keep repeating mental and behavioural patterns learned in childhood which are enforced by our parents, peers, schools and society, we end up feeling dissatisfied with life. In order for our soul to evolve we need to discover our own personal path by tuning in to our inner voice.

Transformation takes place when we become aware of an inner impulse that needs to find outer expression.

Our crystalline planet

Not only can flowers facilitate personal development, they have been, and are, instrumental in changes of consciousness on a global level.

The idea that the earth has an inherent symmetry is a very ancient one. A student of Socrates was told by his master that the earth viewed from above looks like a ball made out of twelve pieces of skin sewn together. Two thousand years later, some Russian scientists decided to re-examine the earth to see whether it had any significant symmetrical patterns. Their findings were published in Moscow in *Khimiya I Zhizn*, a popular science journal published by the USSR Academy of Sciences. The title of the paper was 'Is the earth a giant crystal?'

I have already hinted that during the formation of our earth, a matrix of cosmic light energy could have been embodied into the structure of the earth itself. A crystal formation is, in fact, revealed if you divide the earth in the manner described by Socrates. The surface of the globe can be divided exactly into twelve pentagonal slabs forming a dodecahedron. Onto this we can then overlay 20 equilateral triangles, marking each crystal facet.

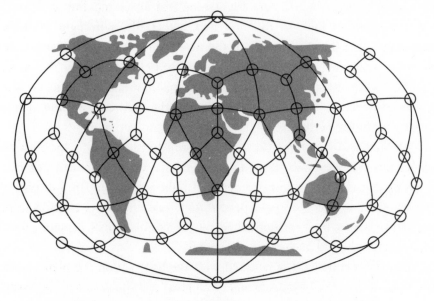

'Is the Earth a large crystal?' – the Soviet illustration as it appeared in *Khimiya I Zhizn*

At the points where the slabs of triangles meet are areas of great magnetic energy and it is often at these places that we find geographical fault-lines, sites of ancient civilisations, magnetic disturbances and places of spiritual importance.

With the passing of time, the continental drift has altered the symmetry of the crystal, so that the powerful cosmic forces are not flowing freely as before. The Russian scientists also believe the energy in the crystalline pattern is not constant, but ebbs and flows in rhythmic cycles, according to its own internal mathematical harmony.

The significance of this is beginning to reveal itself with the coming of the new millennium and the astrological changes that are taking place during this time. Astrologically speaking, we are moving into the solar civilisation from the Piscean age into the Aquarian age. Our present planetary rulers are Uranus and Saturn, which contain the energy to bring change and the unexpected into our lives. These planets will have a strong planetary influence until the year 2190.

Healing for the new era

Before a new order can take form, the old one has to be broken down, and we can see this happening in the world today. Old ideals and standards are fast disappearing, which is very frightening and unsettling, but we have to move forward to look to the new and higher ideals brought with the Aquarian Age. With the coming of the new millennium, great changes are likely to occur in our needs and levels of consciousness. It is the subtle healing systems using cosmic energy such as colour, sound, and other electro-magnetic vibrations that will be able to offer the right type of approach to healing for future needs.

With these major astrological changes, a new form of healing for both the planet and its life are also taking form. These are the development of flower essences that reflect the cosmic energy of light and colour. In a display of synchronicity all over the world, people are developing flower essences using the native plants that are nourished by the cosmic forces of sun, moon, planets and stars and magnetic earth energy.

When the cosmic light is reunited with the light within the planet itself, the force field of energy created will be so great that the power of the earth's crystal energy will be restored. When this happens great healing will take place that will free us from distortions in physical energy and we will be able to make a major leap forward in the evolution of our consciousness.

In the following table I have laid out some of the flower-essence ranges that are being developed around the world. If we lay a grid showing the crystalline structure of the earth over a map of the world, we can see some of the major intersections coincide with areas where flower essences are being developed.

AREA	Latitudes in degrees	FLOWER ESSENCES OF THE WORLD
SOUTHERN	20–40 south	Australian Bush, Living Essences – Australia, New Zealand, Cape (South Africa)
EQUATOR	20 south – 0–20 north	Rainforest, Brazil, Hawaiian, Arizona
NORTHERN	20–40 north	Bach Flowers, Master's flower essences California, Perelandra, FES (Flower Essence Society)
NORTHERN	40–55 north	Pacific Sea and Flower, Findhorn Flower and Bailey Flower, AUM Himalayan Slanjeevini Essences, Bloesem Remedies Netherlands
ARCTIC	55–80 north	Alaskan Flower and Environmental Essences

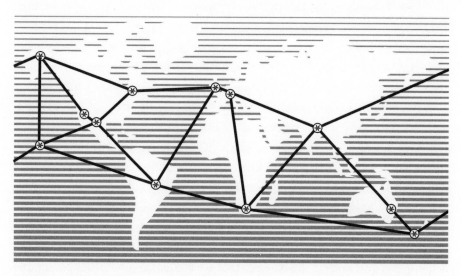

The lines of the grid form crystalline structures which also pass through areas where flowers grow. The points of intersection fall through the following places:

Alaska, Canada, California, Nevada, Arizona, New Mexico, Porto Rico (The Bahamas), Brazil, Peru, Sahara, West Africa, South Africa, Scotland, Egypt, Ukraine, New South Wales and Northern Territory (Australia), Himalayas (Tibet), Thailand, Indonesia. Lines also pass through France, Spain, India and Sri Lanka so I would expect that further flower and vibrational essences will be developed in these areas.

The spiritual renaissance

It is a paradox that the art of living depends on our ability to strike a balance between two opposites: the physical and the spiritual realms. In order to create this harmony we need to rediscover a sense of sacred in all that surrounds us.

We live in an age when we tend to believe that science can provide us with all the answers. It is helpful to remember that it was Albert Einstein himself who understood the close connection between wonder and the sacred. To him the sense of wonder was the most important sense to open ourselves to the truth: the mystery and divinity of ourselves and the world.

This spontaneous development of flower healing all over the world indicates more than mere coincidence. There appears to be a divine force working behind the scenes. This appearance of the right information at just the right time marks the fact that we are, indeed, undergoing a new spiritual renaissance. There seems to be a deep desire to discover a heightened spiritual perception in everyday life, so that the divine becomes a tangible and real experience. This desire for spirituality is different from the renaissance of the past as it transcends all religious doctrine and cultures.

In the past we have interacted with the world in an arrogant and external way. We have moved and reorganised nature to suit not only our needs but our desires, and if we continue to pursue this destructive route the earth will no longer be able to sustain life. As we cannot replace resources that we have destroyed we need to find another way of restoring balance to the sensitive eco-systems. Manipulation of the physical world is no longer an option and we must look towards a more fundamental way of changing our relationship with the earth. It is only through out own spiritual evolution that we can achieve this and reverse the damage that we are causing both the planet and ourselves. It is quite clear that humankind will repeat the errors of the past unless there is an upward leap in our own consciousness which will make us fully responsible for our actions and their consequences. In order to restore harmony to our planet we have to work both individually and as a group. It is the time in our evolution when, like flowers, we must reverse the energy from an inward to an outward flow. We have to move from a position of taking to that of giving.

If we believe that our universe came into being by accident we will not recognise a power greater than ourselves. After all, it is as unlikely that life came into being by chance as it would be for a whirlwind to rush through a junk yard and assemble Concord. It is through a more subtle interaction with the natural kingdoms on earth that we can experience a feeling of inner connection with the divine intelligence in the universe.

The gift of flowers allows us to experience a greater sense of the sacred harmony in and around us. This understanding imbues us with energy, well-being and wisdom. By using the ancient knowledge of the floral kingdom we can come to understand ourselves better. By developing our individual sensitivity and intuition, we can work together to make the world a better place.

Flower Reading Chart

For: _____

Date: _____

Flower chosen: (If you do not know the name of the flower, write a brief description) _____

Description of your flower and where it was found:

_____

_____

Flower family – Central theme

_____

_____

Habitat and growth pattern – Your present state of being and circumstances

_____

_____

Shape of flower – Signifies any area of disharmony

_____

_____

Healing vibration and purpose of the flower

Number of petals: _____

Colour: _____

Texture: _____

Aroma: _____

Insect energy: _____

Special messages:

_____

_____

Further reading and useful addresses

The healer's manual: A beginner's guide to energy therapies by Ted Andrews (1993), Llewellyn Publications, USA

The language of flowers by Kristyna Artcati (1997), Headway – Hodder and Stoughton

Discovering the folklore of plants by Margaret Baker (1928), Shire Publications Ltd

Colour scents by Suzy Chiazzari (1998), The C.W. Daniel Company

Insects and flowers – a biological relationship by John Brackenbury (1995), Blandford Books

The plant: Volumes 1 & 2 by Gerbert Grohmann (1974), Bio-dynamic Gardening and Farming Assoc.

The encyclopaedia of flower remedies by Clare Harvey and Amanda Cochrane (1995), Thorsons

Flower essences of Alaska by Steve Johnson (1992), Alaskan Flower Essence Project, Homer

Flowers that heal – How to use flower essences by Patricia Kaminski (1998), Newleaf, Dublin

Findhorn flower essences by Marion Leigh (1997), Findhorn Press

Flower remedies by Peter Mansfield (1995), Optima

The complete floral healer by Anne McIntyre (1996), Gaia Books

Energy medicine by Sabina Pettitt (1993), Pacific Essences, Victoria, Canada

The Bach Flower Remedies by Nora Weeks and Victor Bullen (1964), The C.W. Daniel Company

The fragrant mind by Valerie Ann Worwood (1995), Doubleday

A prospect of flowers by Andrew Young (1945), Penguin Country Library

Useful addresses

- British Flower and Vibrational Healing Association, 8 Willow Glen, Branton, Doncaster DN3 3JD.
  e-mail: bfvea@greenmantrees.demon.co.uk
- Kirlian and Aura photography: Harry Oldfield, The School of Electro-Crystal Therapy, 17 Long Drive, South Ruislip, Middx HA4 0HL
- International Association of Colour, Cottenham Road, Histon, Cambridge CB4 9ES. Tel: 01223 563403
- The Register of Qualified Aromatherapists, PO Box 6941, London N8 9HF
- Herbal Remedies: Potters Herbal Supplies Ltd, Leyland Mill Lane, Wigan, Lancashire WN1 2SD. Tel: 01942 234761
- Dr Edward Bach Centre, Mount Vernon, Sotwell, Wallingford, Oxfordshire, OX10 0PZ

Flower essence producers

- Healing Herbs, PO Box 65, Hereford HR2 0DX
- Mail order suppliers of Flower and Vibrational Essences: IFEP, The Living Tree, Liphook, Hants GU30 7JS. Tel: 01428 741572
  e-mail: flowers@atlas.co.uk
- Flower and Gem Remedy Assoc., Site 1, Castle Farm, Glifton Road, Deddington, Oxon OX15 0TP

Training courses

- The Iris International School of Colour Therapy which is run by the author, Suzy Chiazzari, offers home study courses and workshops in various topics including vibrational medicine, colour, gem and flower essences and healing gardens.

A set of flower cards designed for the purpose of giving flower readings is also available.

Iris International, Farfields House, Jubilee Road, Totnes, Devon TQ9 5BP, UK.
e-mail: iris@eclipse.co.uk Tel: 01803 868 037 Fax: 01803 866 079

Index

Note: page references in italic refer to illustrations

acacia 9

acupuncture and acupressure 70, 85

aloe 35, 50

angelica 48

angel's trumpet 51

Aquarian age 112

aromatherapy vii

arrogance 45

astilbe 53

aura imaging and photography 16, 70–1

Australian aborigines 108

Babylonia 55

Bach, Edward (Dr) 10–11, 17, 18, 39, 65

   Dr Bach's Rescue Remedy 77

balance 57, 69, 114

bees 35, 45, 53, 58, 73

birds 10, 13

bleeding heart 42

blood cleansing 47

bluebell and bluebell family 32, 42

body language 39

body, mind and spirit 56, 57

borage 41, 74

brain and brainwaves 26, 49, 57, 75

breathing technique 22, 26, 27

broom 44

Brown, Pam 7

buddleia 53, 83

bulrush 75, 96–8

burn-out 50

butterflies 23, 95, 101–2

   and buddleia bush 53, 83

   relationship to flowers 58, 59, 60

chakras 15, 16, 57, 67, 80, 85

   base 34, 56, 68

   brow *see* chakras, third eye

   crown 47, 49–50, 69, 81, 90, 101

   and flowers 67–8

   heart 56, 68, 81, 91

   and number of petals 56

   sacral 68, 81

   solar-plexus 57, 68, 81

   third eye 24, 56, 69, 80, 101

   throat 46–7, 51, 68–9

chamomile 33, 77

character viii, 4, 8–10, 88, 90

cherry 9

China and Chinese 54, 57, 70

Chinese lantern 54
chrysanthemum 46
Churchill, Winston 4
climate and character 88
clover 48
colours and colour energy 35,
    69–73, 90
  and flower healing 71–2
  and geography 87
  and life themes 72–3
  see also flowers, colour
columbine 54
confidence and security 32
communication 32, 35, 46–7, 50, 51, 72
  and flower essences 90
  and looking inwards 66
  between plants and animals 10,
    38, 70
compassion 58
complementary medicine 13
convolvulus family 51
cosmic organisation 11, 15, 57, 107,
    112
cosmos (plant) 46
coughs and colds 51
courage 32
creepers 50, 51
  see also flowers,climbers
cycles of nature 3, 66, 78, 82, 87, 112

daffodil 8, 33, 51
daisies and daisy family 33, 46, 66
damselfly 98
Dante 7
death 33, 46, 51
decision-making 54
delphinium 81

Deva 13, 26, 61, 77, 83, 85
  communication with 10, 23–5, 27,
    30, 73
disease 10–11, 16–17
divine proportions 56
doctrine of signatures 11, 24, 39
dolphins 5
dreams 54, 79

earth 102, 112
  as a crystal 111, 112–14
  healing of 105–7
  relationship with human body
    105–7
  and sunlight 107–8
echinacea 45
Egypt 9, 31
Einstein, Albert 114
elements, five natural 57, 92–3
empathy 58
energy 48, 65–6
  blocked 41–2, 47, 49, 69, 89
  centres of body 15–16
  cosmic 15, 107, 112
  healing viii, 56, 57, 77
  interchange 23–4
  life-force 56, 58, 66
  movement and flow 66, 70–1
  of numbers 55
  and planetary forces 56, 57
  raising of level 40–1, 49
energy medicine 14–15
energy patterns 66
  decoding 26–7
  and geographical location 89
  and inner state 28–9
  and petals 29, 55–8

eucalyptus 74, 76
evening primrose 43
evolution 5–8, 110–11
    spiritual 7, 108
eye problems 49

fairy lantern 42
families of flowers 29–36
feminine principle 31, 42, 48, 51, 102
    and blue flowers 72
    and number 57, 58
    and tiger lily 47, 99, 100
ferns 5, 91
feverfew 48
fire 52
fleur-de-lis 9
flexibility 44
flower ceremonies 78–80
flower essence 16–17, 80–92, 95
    auras 87
    choice of 88–9
    commercially made 85–6, 92
    creating 80–4
    and earth's structure 113–14
    geographical location 86, 90–2
    taking (dosage) 84–5
    for travellers 89–90
flower psychometry 6–7, 18
    definition 4
    and illustrations 25–6, 60
    and intuition 22
flower readings 12
    case studies 83–102
flowermancy see flower psychometry
flowers
    aroma 51, 54, 58, 95, 97, 99
        and attraction 18, 24

    and colour 75–7
    and communication 10, 70
    and energy patterns 66, 71–2
    and evolution 108
    and geography 106
    and healing 26, 65, 75–7, 95, 101
    and texture 73–4
choice of 21–2, 25–6
climbers 38, 101
colour 24, 42, 56, 58, 67, 108
    and anger 99
    and aroma 75–7
    and chakras 67
    and communication 10, 70
    and evolution 108
    and geography 87, 90–2, 106,
        107
    and healing 26, 65, 66, 74, 95,
        97
    and life themes 72–3, 109
    and message 31, 50
    and purity 56
    and spirituality 48, 101
and energy 17, 66–7, 71, 77
and five elements 92–3
geographical location of 88–9,
    92–3, 106
    hot, dry regions 91
    polar 90, 106
    temperate 91–2
    tropical 90–1
and growth stage 108–9
habitat 31, 36–8, 67, 94, 99
    dry and arid 37, 74
    sunny 37
hanging 37–8
healing properties of 10, 65, 77, 87
illustrations of 22, 76

and intuitive relationship 7
key-notes 30
language 3
and national character 8–10
shapes 39–55, 67, 108
  bell shape 41–2
  candle or flame 52–3
  cap or crescent 46–7
  cup shape 42–3
  drooping sprays 44–5
  radiating petals 45–6
  spikes 49–50, 96
  star shapes 40–1, 75
  symbolic forms 53–5
  trumpet 50–1, 99
  umbels and clusters 47–8, 94,
    100–1
single and double 37
small 37
and spiritual growth 28
structure 12, 28–9
texture 26, 73–5, 95, 97, 99, 101
and ultra-violet light 73
vibrations 16
foxglove and foxglove family 35, 53
fuchsia 37–8, 41–2

'Gaia' 88–9
gardens 7, 10, 18, 29, 47, 54
  and choice of flower 21
garlic 49
grace 33–4
grasses 45, 75
grasshopper 59
Greece 55
Grohmann, Gerbert 105–6
growth and maturation 72–3

habitat *see* flowers, habitat
harmony viii, ix, 57, 69
  and health 10–11, 14
headaches 49
healing *see* flowers, healing
  properties of
heart 34, 53, 56
hibiscus 9, 30, 81
hollyhock 30
homoeopathy vii, 13
honeysuckle 35, 38, 54, 100
hydrangea 94–6

India 9, 16, 55, 67
indian paintbrush 53
innocence 33
insects 10, 13, 43, 73
  energy 58–61, 95, 97, 100, 101, 102
  and flower readings 58, 95
inspiration 31
intuition 27, 42, 58, 73, 83
  and inner guidance 47, 74
iris and iris family 31, 41, 54–5, 181

Johnson, Steve 85

Kepler, Johann 107–8
Kirlian photography 70–1

lady's slipper 34
lavender 49, 74, 77
Leonardo da Vinci 5
lethargy 51, 53
life and life-force 66, 72–3, 80, 81, 107

light 90
  see also sunlight
lilies and lily family 31, 55, 77
  see also tiger lily
location of flowers *see*
    flowers,habitat
lotus 9, 58, 81
love 43, 52, 53, 54, 91
  and flower essences 78, 82
  and lotus flower 58, 81
  and rose family 30–1, 81

mandalas 67–8, 80
marigold 46
marjoram 8, 77
masculine principle 57, 102
meadowsweet 74
meditation 67, 80, 102
  and flower essences 83, 85
  and healing vii, 77, 79
mental exhaustion 47
Mercury (planet) 55
mimicry 13, 34, 38–9, 58, 91
mind 22, 56, 57
mind-body connection 16–17
Monk's hood 47
moon 82, 90
moths 43, 54, 58, 60, 101–2
mullein 52
music 9, 87, 98, 100, 107–8

narcissus 8, 52, 55
nasturtium 47
nervous system and problems 32, 43,
    49, 76
numbers and energy 55–8

orchids and orchid family 10, 33–4,
    91

pampas grass 96–8
Paracelcus 13
peppermint 30, 50, 76
petals 29, 55, 75, 78, 79–80
phantom leaf and limb 70–1
planets 107, 112
  and healing 55–8, 105–7
poppy 9, 43
protea 9, 43
psyche viii, 4, 8–10, 88, 90
purity 53, 56

red hot poker 52
reflexology and reflexes 70, 85
relaxation 44
rose and rose family 7, 8, 30–1, 76, 81
Ruskin, John vii

sage 49–50
St John's Wort 41
sandalwood 76, 77
scent *see* flowers, aroma
security 32
self-awareness 45
self-confidence 9, 32, 45, 73, 94
self-expression 9, 46–7, 50
self-love 52
sensitivity 32, 48
sexuality 42, 89, 91, 100
shamrock 9
simplicity 5–7, 33–4
sleep 79

slipper flower 54
snapdragon family 32
snowdrop family 33
Socrates 111
solarisation 11
soul 11, 108
  see also spirituality
spider flower 54
spine 15, 56
spirals 66–7
spirituality 47, 48, 55, 56, 58, 91
  and evolution 108, 114–15
  and geography 88
  realms 51, 55, 74
  renaissance 114–15
stamens 29, 43, 54, 58, 75, 100
Star of Bethlehem 41
stars 90, 112
Steiner, Rudolph 58, 59, 110
stick-insect 59
strength, inner 34
stress 6, 12, 14, 96, 97, 102
study 94, 96
subtle bodies 15, 57, 74, 77
succulents 74
sun 90, 112
sunflower 7, 45, 59, 66, 81
sunlight 37, 89
  and cosmic force 107, 111
  and flower essences 17, 80, 83
  variations in 87
support 94, 96
survival 33
sweet pea 38

telepathy 6
thistle 8, 41, 75

Tibet 67
tiger lily 31, 47, 98–100, 102
Trinity 57
trumpet vine 51
tulip 9, 43

Vedas 16
Venus (planet) 55
'vibrational genetic make-up' 87
vibrations 15–16
  of flower essences 84
  and genetics 87, 88
  healing 11, 12, 15, 17, 77, 82
  and insect visitors to flowers 58–61
  sensitvity towards 6
  sympathetic energy 26, 29
  within plants 16, 65–6
    captured from sunlight 11, 12, 24
vines 38, 50
violets and violet family 32, 77
vision 56
visualisation technique 25, 73
  and chakras 80, 81
  and flower selection 26, 27
  and insect energy 60, 61

willow 44
wisdom 47, 49–50, 73
wisteria 44
Wordsworth, William 13

yarrow 30, 48
yerba santa 51
yoga 58

zinnia 46